The STARS' WAR

foreword by
HRH THE DUKE OF EDINBURGH, KG, KT

OTHER BOOKS BY HUGH MORGAN

"By the Seat of Your Pants!"
The Basic Training of RAF Pilots during World War II.
Foreword by Air Marshal, Sir John Curtiss. Newton, 1990.

Forthcoming Title:
Adults with Autism.
Cambridge University Press. Due 1994.

The STARS' WAR

foreword by
HRH THE DUKE OF EDINBURGH, KG, KT

Edited by Hugh Morgan

Published in 1993 by The S.P.A.
in conjunction with
Oakfield House Publications
6-12 Oakfield Road,
Selly Park,
Birmingham.

British Library Cataloguing in Publication Data

A catalogue record for this book is available
from the British Library

ISBN 1 85421 222 2

Designed and Produced by Images Ltd.
Front cover by Chris Redman and illustrations by Kevin Hayes.
Printed and Bound in Great Britain.

ACKNOWLEDGEMENTS

The cause of autism has benefited greatly from the support of numerous celebrities who have contributed their recollections to *The Star's War*. To those household names, Oakfield House Publications and the West Midlands Autistic Society Ltd, are extremely grateful. Additionally, in the production of this book other people have played highly significant roles, namely The Duke of Edinburgh for his foreword, and Jill Nowell, Kevin Hayes, Tony Mullins of Oakfield House; Tony Harold, Sue Wilson, Cintia Stammers, and especially Chris Redman for his excellent art work, of Images Publishing (Malvern) Ltd. Appreciation is due to John Golley for his advice and suggestion of the title. Particular thanks are also due to Dame Jill Knight M.P. for her valuable support in the launch of *The Stars' War* at the House of Commons.

Every effort has been made to trace the copyright owners of all extracts included in *The Stars' War* and wish to express appreciation to the following:

Cliff Michelmore and Jean Metcalf – *Two Way Story* – Hamish Hamilton;

Brian Johnston – *It's Been a Lot of Fun* – W.H.Allen;

George Melly – *Rum/Bum Concertina* – Weidenfeld & Nicholson;

Derek Jameson – *Touched by Angels* – Random Century;

Michael Bentine – *The Door Marked Summer* – Grafton Books Publishing Ltd;

Spike Milligan – *Mussolini – His part in my downfall* – Penguin Books;

David Tomlinson – *Luckier than Most* – Hodder and Stoughton;

Donald Sinden – *Touch of the Memoirs* – Hodder and Stoughton;

Harry Secombe – *Arias and Raspberries* – Robson Books;

Denis Healey – *The Time of my Life;*

Michael Denison – *Overtures and Beginners* – Victor Gollancz Ltd;

Richard Todd – *Caught in the Act – Story of My Life* – Random Century Hutchinson;

David Jacobs – *Jacobs Ladder;*

Jon Pertwee – *Moon Boots and Dinner Suits* – Elmtree;

Brian Rix – *My Face from My Elbow;*

Max Bygraves – *After Thoughts* – W.H. Allen.

CONTENTS

FOREWORD

H.R.H. The Duke of Edinburgh, K.G. K.T.

                    BUCKINGHAM PALACE.

The saying goes that 'all's fair in love and war'.
This also applies to fund-raising for charities. There
can be no doubt that Oakfield House Autistic Community
provides an invaluable service, but, like all good
charities, it needs funding. Hugh Morgan has hit on a
splendid idea and I hope that this book will prove to
be sufficiently popular to bring in some much needed
funds for the West Midlands Autistic Society.

Readers may find their credulity stretched by some
of the stories, but they should remember the other
saying that 'truth is stranger than fiction'. I suspect
that this book will prove that to be the case.

1992

NORMAN WISDOM

I'll be for the High Jump

It was when I was serving as a fifteen year old Band Boy in the Tenth Royal Hussars in India (I joined when I was fourteen), that it all happened, and when I say all I mean all.

I owe everything to the " Shiney Tenth", as they were known. I learnt music, how to play several instruments, singing and dancing. I played clarinet and saxophone in the Band, Violin in the String Orchestra. I enjoyed football, cricket, swimming and became Fly Weight Boxing Champion of The British Army in India. That's eight stone and I'm not much more now. I was soon enlisted as full member of the concert party. It was undoubtedly the happiest time of my life. One of the important things that led to my becoming a professional comedian when I was demobbed, was the fact that I was mad on gymnastics and learnt how to fall without hurting myself. The following anecdote is an amusing example that I shall never forget.

Having passed out of riding school, it was customary to go out in the early morning for a free will canter. At the same time, we would exercise horses who had no riders available at that time. I had been lumbered with two exercise horses, one on either side, whilst in centre I rode my beloved horse No. 16,

"Pretty Bitch", as I used to call her.

It was not unusual for the Rough Riding Sgt. Major Turner, who was in charge, to shout "Follow me", and as he dashed off on his horse in his self chosen direction, there would be screams of laughter and fear, plus a considerable amount of abuse as we endeavoured to do so. Over rough ground, ditches, through low trees, over hedge rows etc., and this is when it happened. I headed for the hedge at full gallop, with the accompanying exercise horses held firmly by their reigns in either side. The intention was, that we would all jump together but alas, this was not to be the case. My beloved horse "Pretty Bitch" refused to jump, and as the two exercise horses took off I was dragged high into the air holding on to the reigns and, with the exception of "Pretty Bitch", we cleared the hedge comfortably.

Sadly, I didn't land as skilfully as my two exercise horses. I think it must have been one of the loudest laughs I have ever heard in my life, including any theatre audience. I didn't look upon it as amusing at the time, but I certainly can't help laughing now, or on the many occasions when I visualise it again from the point of view of my colleagues, and in particular my Rough Riding Sgt. Major Turner.

VICTOR MADDERN

I Give You One Wish

I was fourteen years old when my Fairy Godfather granted me one wish, so I . . . but I must begin at the beginning.

I started work as a lowly office boy in the shipping company, Runciman (London) Ltd, owners of the Anchor Line. Sir Philip Runciman was a courteous and kindly man; as I entered his room, he held out the enamelled mug and said "I wonder if you would be so kind as to go across the road to the Aerated Bread Company and get me a cup of coffee?" He held out a threepenny piece and I departed on the errand. It occurred to me that I could improve on this routine. The next morning, I risked my own threepence, and collected the coffee at 8.58, then followed Sir Philip up the stairs, coffee mug in hand. When he summoned me, I went in and placed the mug on his desk.

"Your coffee, Sir Philip."

"Good gracious! Thank You!" There was a pause. "You're new, aren't you? What is your name?"

"Maddern, Sir."

"Well, Mr Maddern, do you know, you are the first boy in over forty years to bring my coffee without being asked. I like that. It shows initiative. Now, if there is anything you want –

anything – come and ask me. If it is at all possible, I will help you. And here is your threepence. Thank you very much."

"Thank *you*, Sir Philip."

I was in no hurry to make use of my wish; it was too good to waste. Then one day, a very handsome, very young man walked into the office in what looked like a naval officer's uniform. I learned from his conversation with the lady telephonist that he was Mr Mungo, the Senior Cadet from the company's Capital Ship, the *SS California*, which had just been sunk.

Now I knew how I would use my wish; I wanted to be like Mr Mungo.

As I write this, I have just looked at the clock and the calendar; it is forty-nine years to the hour since I boarded *SS Nea Hellas* at mid-day, December 3rd, 1943, in my brand-new officer's uniform, carrying my bag full of a complete rig-out bought and paid for by Sir Philip. I had convinced myself and my family that this was the life for me; I hated every second of it.

I had not been at sea many days when I discovered my cap tended to ride down to the left side of my head. I was puzzled. I gently investigated the back of my neck. There, protruding above the collar, was a large lump. I felt no pain; just panic. I stopped looking for U-boats, I stopped looking for anything. I succumbed to my sea-sickness and asked permission to leave the bridge. Captain James McGill Brown ('My name is not a name – it's a Nation') roared with laughter. "That'll teach you to listen to your mother," he shouted. I took a dive for the companionway down to my cabin. I was followed by the voice of Captain James McGill Brown bellowing orders to the junior assistant second mate, "Force something down him and tell him never to be sick on an empty stomach." The Second was kind with his help and generous with the fatty pork sandwich he made me eat in the lavatory.

Three days later I woke up in North Africa. The lump stayed with me and so did my secret; at least I thought it was a secret.

I made several trips with Lumpy. Around the time that I began to feel a little pain, I was called up onto the bridge of the *Nea Hellas*, or "Nellie Wallace". She was the sister ship of the *California*, and I was very proud and very fond of her. We four cadets were lined up and the Mate walked around us. "Captain Blair has been given his first command. She is an American liberty ship, one of those welded jobs! Which of you would like to join her? . . . Jenkins? Um?" "No, thank you sir." "Bowie?" "I'd rather stay here, sir." "What about you, McLauchlan?" "If it's all the same to you, sir, I am quite happy where I am." The Mate made off towards the wheelhouse. "Get your bags packed, Maddern, and leave your cabin tidy."

I had the bonus of two week's leave and eventually joined the *SS Samvannah* in Newcastle. She was tiny. So tiny she did not even have a ship's doctor. The Canadian Mate, Mr George, was very direct, very fair but not over fond of cadets. I overheard him telling the story of finding a box by his bunk-side marked 'Ship's Doctor', and a booklet telling how to perform an appendectomy in an emergency. I decided to keep my lump to myself a bit longer.

When we got into the Red Sea the pain began to get much worse and finally it was noticed that I was walking more and more with my head tilted to the right and backwards. "What's the matter with your neck?" asked Captain Blair. He had been the Staff Captain on the Nellie Wallace and was a kind, gentle soul.

17

"I've got a boil, sir, I think."

"Let me see!" He walked around to the back to me. "A boil! More like a carbuncle! Has Mr George seen it?"

"No, sir."

Captain Blair looked at me in surprise, "Why not? Go and let him have a look at it." That was the first bit of sympathy I had received since I had discovered Lumpy.

I knocked on the Mate's door. "Yes, what is it?" The door remained shut.

"I've got a pain in my neck, sir."

He came out into the dimly lit passageway and looked at my neck. He took me into his cabin and began to tell me how there was a way of heating a bottle with steam and placing it on the carbuncle or boil so that, as the temperature in the bottle decreased, the suction power of the bottle opening would increase and cause a vacuum. "That's how they did it in the sailing ship days." he said. I was quick to remind him that this was a steam ship – and new. "I'll show you how new she is," he said, lifting up an ominous looking wooden box. "This is the Ship's Doctor's box." He put the box down again and then said that he had spotted Lumpy almost before he had spotted me. "I have got something called a kaolin poultice." He told me all about it and about how, so uncomfortable would it become bandaged around my neck in the tropics, that I would eventually beg him to operate on me.

"No, sir, I'll be alright. I am a very hot-blooded person. Heat does not bother me, Sir."

He began to prepare the poultice and murmured, "We'll see. "

A long time later and after many visits to Mr George's cabin, we led the way into Singapore. We had on board the only living

18

Pilot who knew the way back. The *SS Samvannah* proudly steamed into the harbour ahead of perhaps a hundred ships: big ones, small ones, troop carriers and cargo vessels of all the Allied nations. Directly astern of us was the giant Royal Navy cruiser, *HMS Cleopatra*. She tied up astern of us too and then sent up a glorious array of signal flags. They were not just decoration to cheer up the prisoners of war that had been released and were on the dockside to welcome us in. In fact there were many messages there and one was to announce that she was the official Hospital Ship. The Mate saw this as his opportunity.

"Maddern. Do you know how to salute a Royal Navy ship's officer?" I admitted I did not. You did not do that sort of thing in the Merchant Navy.

"You see the *Cleopatra*? Well, she's the official Hospital Ship. That means she'll be swarming with experts on carbuncles. Get below and put on your clean whites." He told me to clean my shoes like they had never been cleaned before. "Make them respect us when you go aboard that cruiser. And remember, you salute the Quarter Deck; that little spot where Nelson died. It's symbolic! You will recognise the Officer of the Watch by the telescope under his arm. He will return the salute . . ." My head began to swim. When I was dressed I reported to Mr George and he duly inspected me. My ears, fingernails, shirt collar, buttons, clean handkerchief, inside my pockets, everything. We rehearsed several times.

I walked behind the warehouses between me and *HMS Cleopatra*. I recalled being sent to the Ministry of Transport in Berkeley Square, wearing a newly acquired army cadet uniform without the Army Cadet battledress marking. I remembered a Major in battledress, a Red Beret on his head. I did not know how to salute so I blew my nose as I passed, pretending I had not seen him. I remembered the dig in the ribs and the anguished shout: . . . "You! Salute when you see an Officer . . . Go on . . . Salute damn you!"

I had a handkerchief in one hand and a large 'Top Secret' parcel in the other. My parcel for the Ministry of War Transport was much more important than the two of us put together. In any case I was not in His Majesty's Forces, I was only a trainee trumpet player in the junior army cadet brass band. "Salute, damn you, salute!" Another dig in the ribs and I doubled up. The Top Secret envelope went flying. The whole of Berkeley Square stood still. It was like 11a.m. on the 11th November. Two minutes' silence with everybody looking at the gallant officer and the insubordinate private refusing to pay his respects. My handkerchief went up in the air like a white flag of surrender and down came my salute . . . sort of. "That's better." I tried to tell him that I was not a real soldier. "You're damned right you are not. Think yourself lucky I am in a hurry or I would have you clamped in irons." All these thoughts began flooding back to me as I made my way across the back of the warehouses. I was still only seventeen. Was this pretty uniform really worth it? If only I had waited for Sir Philip Runciman to press the buzzer for his coffee . . .

I rounded the warehouse and there I saw my first dilemma. Which of the two gangplanks led to the Quarter Deck where Nelson died? I looked up and saw two rows of RN sailors with fixed bayonets at the head of one gangway and two rows of Royal Marines at the other. I took the first gang plank and there by the grace of God was an Officer with a telescope. At the first sight of me the Bosun had begun to pipe me aboard. Mr George had said nothing about how to whistle back to them.

I reached the top of the gangway breathless. I saluted, quite well, I thought. The Officer of the Watch came towards me smiling and saluted me! "Good morning, sir. What can we do for you?" I turned my neck to show him Lumpy. "I was wondering, that is, The Mate was wondering . . ." "Green!" he shouted.

"Sir!" The rating came noisily to attention beside us.

"Take this officer down to medical."

"Sir! Follow me please sir!"

It was a long way down. We arrived in the hospital quarters where already doctors were at work on the poor ex-prisoners.

The young doctor who looked at my problem told me it was not quite ready to lance. I heaved a sigh of relief. "I'll tell you what I'll do," he said,'. "I'll give you a kaolin poultice. Do you know what that is?"

"Yes," I assured him.

"Well, if you keep this poultice on until this evening I reckon it should be nice and ripe for me to lance. Can you keep it hot all day? Have you got a large tea urn in the Officer's mess?" I nodded. "Good. Well, every time it cools off, wrap it around the tea urn 'till it gets hot again. Then I would like to see you back here at 6.30. Is that alright? I nodded again. "OK. then. 6.30. Not five thirty or seven thirty." I looked him squarely in the eye and said, "I can tell the time, sir, if I can do nothing else, I can tell the time."

"It's just that it is very important on this occasion." I'd had no idea that surgery was such a precise science. I carefully heated my poultice when necessary.

By six fifteen I was ready. At six twenty five I set off. I stood at the rear of the warehouse and waited until a half minute before six thirty, then rounded the corner and approached *HMS Cleopatra*. To my horror, they had laid a red carpet down for me and what sounded like several pipes piping me aboard. I just could not take it. I quickly withdrew to my warehouse hideaway, my heart thumping. I checked my watch – six thirty three! I decided to have another go. The same thing happened and once more I lost courage and withdrew. By six thirty-seven or thereabouts I was hopelessly confused so I went for bust. Round the corner of the warehouse I went with a very determined stride and up towards the red carpet. Nothing was going to stop me now. I walked up the red carpeted gangway with Lord Louis Mountbatten of Burma.

Later I learned something that made me wonder how we ever won the war in the Far East. We were on three separate timings. Summer Time, Double Summer Time, and some were even on Treble Summer Time.

Years later I was working on a film with Alec Guinness and Dirk Bogarde. The producer was Lord Brabourne better known as John. His father-in-law came out to spend a holiday in Spain and to see some of the filming. It was fun saying to him, "The last time we met was walking up the gangway of *HMS Cleopatra* together."

Donald Pleasence

Be Prepared

A blue sky. Burning, the aeroplane had fallen away – I could see no other parachute, although I knew I was the only one to jump. I was very lonely, very frightened. I think I had pulled the cord too soon.

My parachute had caught on the fuselage and I was going down too fast (it seemed to me). Little puffs of smoke exploded all around. They had got rid of the aeroplane and were having a go at me.

Until some minutes before, I had been a WOP/AG in a Lancaster bomber. This means "Wireless Operator, Air Gunner". The daylight operation was unusual. We normally flew at night at high altitudes and without pressurisation. Communication between crew members was by radio mike, and sometimes these would mist over and freeze up. It was my job to protect the crew's microphones, and I did this with thin squares of rubber which I cut from the prophylactics readily obtainable at the Guard-room. My battledress pockets were full of these condoms, cut into squares, or nestling in their little packets.

Bump! I hit the ground. A perfect Summer's day in France, except that Germans were advancing on all sides, armed with guns, sticks, hammers, pickaxes. Their leader was young, blond, a perfect Aryan, pistol in his hand.

"Pick up your parachute and follow me!" he said. "Pick it up yourself," I said, experiencing a sudden rush of adrenaline. He shouted an order in German. His subordinate came to attention and stretched out his right arm (I had believed it only happened in Pinewood films).

"Heil Hitler!" he cried.

I giggled. It was a mistake. Someone frog-marched me to a small hut. We all crowded inside. I felt very vulnerable. The adrenaline had melted away. The officer began his search. He took my watch, took a few pounds in money and arrived at my battledress top. My secret hoard was thrown on the table. A dozen French letters, some mutilated, some in their packets, some loose. He picked up one by its little rubber end, regarded it in the sunlight.

He smiled. "You vill not be needing zeese!" he said.

BOB MONKHOUSE

A Wartime Memory

Just before the end of August, 1939, my father stood up after Sunday lunch in our Beckenham home and announced to my mother, my brother and me that Hitler was sure to launch massive surprise blitzkrieg upon London, and our house would be in the periphery of it. He told us that he had bought a small house in West Worthing and that we were to move down there at once. I was eleven years old and drew a picture of Hitler on a large piece of paper, cut it into a disc twelve inches in diameter and fixed it under the wire frame of our dartboard. Me and my brother and our darts, we gave Adolf some stick that afternoon.

During the phoney war, that strangely peaceful period that followed the Declaration of Hostilities, I wondered if my father had been right to move us to the South coast. His predicted London blitz wasn't happening, but every Worthing lamppost had placards exhorting residents to "Stay Put". The inference drawn was of invasion, and people were beginning to talk of extended holidays in Scotland and Eire.

One sunny morning in the following July, I sat in our tiny garden composing Christmas card rhymes, simple couplets for which a publisher in Stoke paid a shilling each. The distant pulsing growl of a plane engine made me look up at the sky to see a Dornier-17 bomber flying very low and slowly over the rooftops, heading towards me. The German plane passed directly over my head leaving a sooty trail. I could see the outline of a pilot's helmet as the aircraft swept away, and a few moments later I smelt the oily odour of the smoke. It was as if the plane were lost, seeking some landmark that would give it a reason to choose direction and get away before the RAF came to see what all the noise was about. Even as this thought occurred, two Spitfires came banking down from over the sea, engines grinding out a lighter note than the bomber.

Immediately behind them, higher and in a V formation, three Me-109s appeared like shepherds searching for their lost sheep. All the planes vanished inland and then, lower than ever and with its right engine flickering with little rosy petals of flame, the Dornier returned, heading for the sea time. One of the crew of four was pressed against a glass panel in the bulging forward section and I saw something fall as the pencil-shape body of the fuselage glided away. The RAF and German fighter planes were scribbling angry patterns in the blue high above and the chatter of their guns was surprisingly loud. By this time, I was on my bike, cycling as fast as I could round the little lanes to see if I could find what had fallen from the Luftwaffe bomber. Lots of people were out of their houses, shielding their eyes as they gazed upward. My gaze was downward. I was just twelve and didn't know the impossibly high odds against my finding an unknown object dropped from 150 feet onto a built-up area.

When I saw it lying in the gravel at the edge of a private drive, I recognised it at once. It was a military mess tin, a grey metal box with a lid, intended to carry rations. It was stamped with the outline of a swastika on one side and a spread eagle on the other.

26

Inside it were three photographs, a coloured stone and a letter in German on yellow paper. The photos showed a handsome young man with close-cropped hair and wearing an N.C.O.'s uniform jacket, a pretty young woman posing coyly beside a farm pump, and a fat baby on a rug in a bushy garden. I put the contents back in the box, put it into the basket on my handlebars and cycled home.

I heard later that the Dornier had hit the sea and broken up about two miles off shore. There had been no survivors. No one knew I had the box which I kept wrapped in my winter raincoat at the back of my bedroom cupboard.

Alone in my room at night I pored over the letter, as if sheer concentration would translate its angular German script into a language I could understand. It seemed to be addressed to someone called "Fremde" which I took to be the name of the girl in the photo.

My boyish imagination took wing and I could picture the desperate airman, resigned to a fatal crash, hastily penning this last message of love to his young wife in Germany and then casting it from his dying craft. Entrusting his final words of love to fate, hoping against hope that some intelligent and fearless youngster would find it and devise a way to get it back into the grateful, trembling hands of his beloved Fremde.

Only one teacher at Goring Hall School taught German and was thoroughly hated for possessing such unpatriotic knowledge. He was also given to confiscating any articles he thought unsuitable for children so I was reluctant to show him the original letter. Instead I copied it out, a painstaking task lest I changed the meaning of a word with a clumsily reproduced character. When I thought my final fair copy was as close as I could get to forgery, I took it to Mr Hatfield and asked what it said. He looked at it briefly, put it in his pocket and told me he would see me later about it.

When I got home after school that afternoon I found him and Mr Green, our Headmaster, in our small front room with my mother who was pale with anger. She told me to explain exactly how I had come to write these words on school paper. I blurted out the truth and was sent to bed without supper.

It turned out that the letter was a seditious exhortation to hasten the inevitable Nazi victory by doing all the reader could think of to sabotage the British war effort. The three photographs, said the letter, were typical examples of healthy, strong and friendly German people who wanted only an early end to our hopeless resistance. Ways followed in which the enlightened finder of the letter could aid the German plan to free our precious islands from Jewish and aristocratic domination. Fremde, I learned, was German for "Stranger". The coloured stone, which I had been thinking of swapping for a cap pistol owned by my best friend Docherty, had been enclosed to help finance the subversive deeds, intended to cover the cost of materials needed for train derailment and firesetting new key railway stations. It was a valuable piece of red jasper, dating from Roman times.

My father consulted his solicitor and I was given to understand that the gem had been surrendered to the Crown, whatever that meant. I didn't much care. All I knew was I had a month of extra prep, early bedtime and no going to the Worthing Odeon. Bloody Jerries!

© *Bob Monkhouse, 1992.*

LIONEL JEFFRIES

Fluff

Once upon a-war-time I found myself in Burma as a company commander at the ridiculous age of nineteen. It may be difficult to believe now, but at that time I actually looked "young, pale and interesting", according to a doting mum, but as far as my C.O. was concerned far too young for my own, or the British Army's good. It all came to a head when, on a long march, he heard the men under my command singing "A little child shall lead us".

At the first opportunity he suggested I should make a serious effort to grow a moustache to perhaps avoid such future humiliation. (He also feared that commissioned children might well be a morale booster for any Japanese troops in the area, thus shortening the war to their advantage.)

I concentrated hard and eventually nurtured a pathetic "dead moth" under my nose. I should have got a red star for effort. However, with regular touching up with boot polish, the sprouting took on a king of Ronald Colman elegance. It may have been an ugly "Little Moth" but it was all mine, and I convinced myself that it gave me the necessary age and dignity for the respect I deserved.

Some weeks later, on another trek, the bastards sang "A little child – with a *moustache* – shall lead us!"

Raymond Baxter

Only Owls and Fools Fly at Night

You will rarely hear an RAF pilot speak ill of his aircraft. There are two reasons.

Firstly, it is a matter of professional pride, and secondly one of confidence. Every experienced airman knows that an aeroplane which is unloved is far more likely to kill its pilot than one whose characteristics and temperament are treated with the consideration and tolerance of a lover towards his mistress, however trying that relationship may sometimes be.

Certainly that was true in my day, and even now when the demands of contemporary technology are a quantum leap from those of the Second World War, I discern the same sentiment between today's magnificent men and their flying machines.

Having survived, more-or-less unscathed, two-and-a-half Operational Tours on Spitfires, I will yield to no-one in my love and regard for R.J. Mitchell's masterpiece. But let's face it, the Spitfire was never a good night-fighter. Only desperation could have led to its application to that role.

I admit prejudice. I never really enjoyed night flying. Again there are two reasons. First, the time-honoured adage that "Only birds and fools fly, and birds don't fly at night". Secondly my night vision was the only category in which I ever scored "Below Average". My friends of Bomber Command and others will, of course, laugh this to scorn, and rightly so. But when 65 Squadron was ordered to become 'Night Operational' I, for one, was considerably underjoyed.

At the time we were stationed, appropriately, at Drem in East Lothian, the airfield which had given its name to the historic Drem System of airfield lighting for night flying. The "lights" consisted of paraffin flares which looked like a two gallon teapot with a wick in the spout, and produced a flickering smoky yellow flare about as dim as the proverbial Toc H lamp from which period, I suspect, they dated. They were set out at about 25 yard intervals to mark the line of the grass runway, with a cross-bar to show where you should have landed and a double-flare to tell you that you had gone too far.

I had briefly experienced this primitive arrangement flying Miles Masters at Advanced Flying Training School, and was not impressed. With a Spitfire it was clearly to be a different proposition altogether.

The required sequence of dusk take-offs and landings were no problem. Spitfires had no landing lights, but I could see the ground. But my first Spitfire take-off in total darkness could well have been my last. I did not realise it at the time. In fact, I thought it had gone rather well, and the landing was far better than I had dared to hope.

Imagine my surprise, therefore, when having taxied in without hitting anything, I was told to report immediately to the C.O. – a distinguished French Air Force fighter pilot.

"And what ze 'ell, Baxterre," he said, "do you sink you are doing? You 'ave us all under ze table in Flying Control."

I was flabbergasted. It took me some time to realise what had happened, and when I did, I was too embarrassed to explain.

When I had eased the throttle forward for take-off, I remember being impressed by the violet flames from the exhaust stubs of the Merlin. In daylight I had never seen them before. But as the power increased, and the tail came up, an intermittent stream of yellow sparks added to the fireworks display immediately in front of me. These I had wrongly assumed to be the "goose-neck" paraffin flares of the Drem System flashing past as I accelerated. Consequently, following the sparks from my own exhaust stubs, I had swung right – Spitfires tended to swing on take-off. I cleared the Flying Control Tower by inches, and I remember wondering for a milli-second why it was there!

Those who witnessed it, the C.O. in particular, reasonably assumed that on my first night take-off in a Spitfire, I had executed a "split-arse" turn off the deck in order to "beat-up" Flying Control.

Blatant Irresponsibility. Show-off!

There is not much one can do in such circumstances. I was lucky and I never made that mistake again. There were then, and still are, those less fortunate.

A few months later I volunteered for an "Overseas Posting", went to the North African campaign, joined 93 Squadron and predicated the future pattern of my whole life.

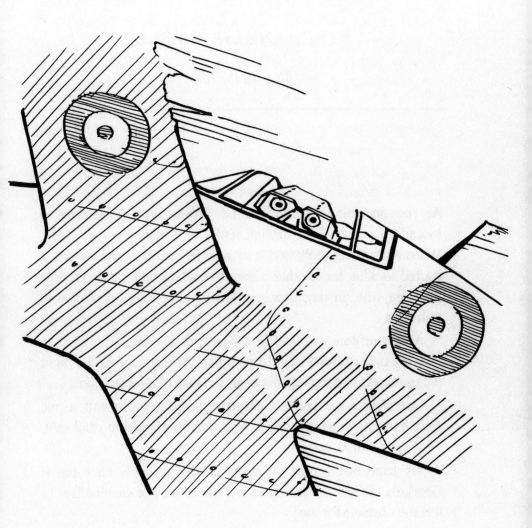

STEPHANE GRAPPELLI

Blues in the Blitz

At the beginning of the Second World War, I worked in Piccadilly as a violinist at Hatchett's, in Arthur Young's band. When Arthur was mobilised, I became the leader of the band and started looking for another pianist to replace him. I met George Shearing who, in those days, played the accordion in a club in Battersea.

After our concerts, and in spite of his blindness, he used to take the underground train to go home. At that time of the night the town was in complete darkness because of the black-out.

One night, I was taking George to the tube station and, as we were hurrying down the street, he suddenly stopped me and said, "Put your arm forward."

My hand met a post which we would certainly have hit, if George's extreme sensitivity to vibrations had not enabled him to feel the obstacle for me.

George Shearing stayed with me for the whole of the war. We played for "the Boys" all over England and Scotland, and gave concerts in hospitals and in military camps. Sometimes we had to play over a background of bomb explosions and air raid warnings. We needed all our courage to play "As Time Goes

By". At one stage we had to recruit discharged musicians in order to keep the band going. And yet, I remember those very painful years as happy years, and still regard England as my second homeland.

MAX BYGRAVES

Blossom

One morning following a concert the night before, I was struck dumb by the gorgeous WAAF Blossom, who came up to me in the mess hall with a request for the words of a song I had vocalised. The song was "If I Had My Way", a big hit with Bing Crosby about that period.

"Of course," I stammered, "I'll be delighted."

She smiled this lovely smile, then turned and walked away with her plate of rissoles and two veg held high so as not to spill the gravy. I couldn't help thinking that if we ever played musical dumplings, she could have my share any time.

I scribbled the words out, put them in my tunic pocket and hoped I would see her soon. It was another week before I bumped into her again, and during that time she had added two stripes to her uniform, so she was now Corporal Murray. Funny how the higher rank of corporal made me, an AC 2, feel so inferior.

"I wrote the words of that song out for you, corporal," I blurted.

"Words? What words?" I pushed them into her hand, she thanked me, then carried on talking to another airman by the name of Cliff Michelmore (yes, that one). There I stood, nineteen years of age – a failure!

Not too long after this, another concert. As I walked on to the stage, I saw Blossom sitting in the front row. Cliff was nowhere in sight. Blossom was with a companion WAAF we called "Blondie". The song I had chosen to sing was a current hit for Perry Como. Without taking my eyes off her, I stood in the spotlight, then directed every lyric in her direction.

"You came – I was alone – I should have known – you were temptation . . ." She was interested. I went for the big finish, "I'm just a slave, only a slave to you – temptation – I'm your slave . . ."

Without warning, the microphone went dead – the Tannoy came on, a voice boomed, "All personnel report to units immediately – all personnel report to units immediately." No bloody applause – just the noise of five hundred men and women scampering from the concert hall, like a scene from M.A.S.H., as the siren wailed another warning.

I brought up my children never to use the word "hate", a word I think should be deleted from the dictionary, but at that moment I hated that bloody Adolf Hitler.

It wasn't until a few days later, when I was talking to Blondie in the NAAFI canteen, that she mentioned her friend Blossom. "She's taken a real fancy to you."

I almost choked on my Tizer. "Me?" I asked.

She nodded, she had to be kidding. "Yes, you – if you asked her for a date, she'd faint. She talks of nothing else."

There were more than fifteen hundred men on that aerodrome and only thirty WAAFs. Blondie had to be joking, because any WAAF could have the choice of dozens of eager males. I tried to be nonchalant, but as they say – it's hard to be humble . . . It must have been another week later, I was travelling back to camp by tube on the Upminster Line. It was late evening and as the doors of the train opened I saw a girl in uniform step into the carriage. It was Blossom. I stood up and offered her my seat, the train lurched and we fell against each other. Wow! Ten thousand volts went through me.

"Do you mind if I walk you back to your billet?" I asked. Her billet was the other side of the camp, which made it a two or three mile walk back to the quarters where I slept. It was a freezing cold night, both of us were buttoned up in greatcoats. After we had gone through the main guard room, I took her arm, she snuggled up close, and even in that freezing atmosphere it felt like the Sahara.

I shook hands with her at the door – no kiss – no funny stuff, then walked back in the Siberian weather to Elm Park – I was in love. My family, who lived on the second floor of the Buildings, guessed I was in love when they kept seeing my feet go past the window.

JAMES HERRIOTT

The Odd One Out

One of my most vivid memories is of an occasion when, as a budding pilot, I was undergoing intensive drill and P.T. at No. 10 Initial Training Wing at Scarborough.

We did so much P.T. and became so expert in the exercises that it was decided to put on a show for a visiting Air Marshal – not only our flight, but several squadrons performing in unison in the big square in front of the Grand Hotel.

We trained for months for the big day. At first the muscular P.T. sergeant shouted instructions all the time, but as we got better and better all he did was call out "Exercise three" or whatever, and finally he merely sounded a tiny peep on his whistle at the beginning of each exercise.

I must admit that it looked very impressive: hundreds of men in white shorts and singlets swinging away as one in utter silence with the sergeant looking down from the balcony above the doorway of the Grand where the Air Marshal would stand on the day.

At the end of each session we marched silently from the square, but somebody got the idea that it would look good if, at the end of the last exercise, we would count up to five then leap into the air, let out a scream at the top of our voices then run off the square at top speed into the various openings between the hotels.

It looked and sounded marvellous. The mass of white clad men going through the long routine in a cathedral hush then leaping into the air yelling like dervishes before disappearing in moments. Another desirable aspect was that it would prove our latent belligerence. The enemy would have quaked at that chilling sound.

The sergeant had a little trouble with a lad in my flight, a tall, gangling, red-haired youth called Cromarty who stood just a few feet in front of me. Cromarty seemed unable to enter into the spirit of the thing.

"Come on, lad," the sergeant said one day. "Put a bit of devil into it. You're floating up and down there like a ruddy fairy godmother."

Cromarty responded by giving an apologetic hop and a feeble cry, so the sergeant called on one of the other lads to give a truly frightening demonstration. Cromarty seemed to model himself on this and day after day the sergeant kept encouraging him until his leap and yell was as fearsome as any.

The great day dawned with blue skies and warm sunshine. We waited in our silent lines while, on the balcony above, gold braid glinted on the Air Marshal's cap. He stood among a knot of the top brass of Scarborough, while in one corner I could see our sergeant, erect in white flannels.

"Peep!" went the whistle and we were off.

There was something exhilarating about being part of this smooth machine. We had ten exercises to do, and I had a wonderful sense of oneness with the arms and legs moving with mine all around. At the end of the ninth exercise I came to attention, waiting for the whistle. Nothing stirred. The silence was profound. Then from the motionless ranks, as unexpected as an exploding bomb. Cromarty, in front of me, launched himself upwards in a tangle of failing limbs and red hair and unleashed a long, bubbling howl.

Cromarty had made it at last. The only snag was that he was one exercise too soon.

When the whistle went for the last exercise a lot of people

didn't hear it because of the noise, and many others were in a state of shock and came in late. It was a shambles, and the final yell and scuttle a sad anticlimax. I myself, though managing to get a few inches off the ground, was unable to make any sound at all.

I felt for the P.T. sergeant. There was nothing he could do. N.C.O.s weren't even allowed to swear at the men. Later I saw him with Cromarty. He put his face close to the young man's.

"You . . . You . . ." His features worked as he fought for words. "YOU THING, YOU!" Then he walked away with bowed shoulders.

BILL OWEN

Pioneering in Oxfordshire

It was in the Royal Pioneer Corps, stationed in the peace and safety of the Oxfordshire countryside, where on the first cold morning of a temporary posting with a dozen O.R.'s*, I found myself as a Corporal in charge of our working party, shifting coal from railway trucks, as the Duty Sergeant had absented himself to phone H.Q. Well, that was his excuse.

It was during this sudden responsibility that we had a visit from the Brigadier, a tall, understanding gentleman, who enquired as to our welfare and the state of our temporary billets. They were bad, very bad, a draughty, rat infested barn, of which, on behalf of my comrades in arms, I explained thus:

"I wouldn't ask a pig to sleep there, sir!"

This evidently prompted him to immediately inspect said billets and, consequently, led to a hasty and angered visit by our C.O. A nasty little shit, who rained fire and brimstone down upon my head with such remarks as, "If necessary, you will sleep in trenches of blood!" I must confess during this tirade I had visions of an immediate posting to some far flung hotbed of slaughter.

---

* *O.R.'s – Other Ranks*

46

But I was wrong. The first indication was the appearance of Army transport to take us back the two miles we had just had to walk with countless tools and barrows in the half-light of that first morning.

We were then driven to our new billets, a warm welcoming village Community Centre, almost next door to the village pub. Our Commanding Officer was posted elsewhere by the end of the week. I was very popular!

NORMAN VAUGHAN

The Ace Card

I was called up to join the King's Regiment in January 1943. The new intake was mainly from Liverpool and after the initial square bashing, was posted to Gibraltar in the August of that year where I expected to be stationed for the rest of the war, as that is where the Regiment had been stationed for a number of years, guarding a collection of Barbary Apes.

Since the age of thirteen I had been in the theatre as a tap dancer, touring the country with various stage shows. Now that I was in the army I had to be found a job and this is where luck played it's first ace card.

An "ace" card that has followed me all my life.

Not having a trade like most of the lads – electrician, motor mechanic or docker, being a dancer and able to play a guitar – I was told, "Vaughan, you'll join the band – cymbal player."

Now that can't be bad – sitting out the rest of the war in Gibraltar, crashing cymbals. On top of that, in the event of combat, bandsmen were stretcher bearers. Cymbals in one hand, stretcher in the other.

Staying in Gibraltar would do me nicely, it was just like pre-war England, all the shop and street lights were on, no blackout to worry about, playing guitar in the Officers' Mess. Further more, in Gibraltar there was no sweet rationing and as I was more than partial to a bar of milk chocolate, Gibraltar, thank you very much, would do me more than nicely, but I hadn't reckoned with our Commanding Officer.

Our C.O. was a career soldier. It was his real job in peacetime so you can imagine his euphoria now we were at war and ready for the fray. One day he mounted a big parade, everybody was there and he urged us to get ready for the big fight ahead.

"It won't be long now, lads, before we meet the Huns. I want to have a crack at the Boche – and soon."

I thought, "If he's so keen, let him go on his own," from which you'll gather, I wasn't too keen to tackle the foe. I didn't want to know about war. Guns I didn't mind. It was the bullets I didn't like.

Rumours abounded the whole time we were on "The Rock". I'll give you a "for instance". Gossip had it that we were going to either North Africa or Italy. After all we'd only left Blighty a couple of weeks earlier and had spent a lot of time jumping in and out of army lorries, wading through streams and filling sandbags, so it was obvious we were soon to be cannon and machine gun fodder, when our C.O., the very same feller who wanted to get his hands on the Huns, was seen buying bananas in Main Street. As bananas were impossible to get in England during the war, it was obvious to all that we were to return home. The rumour went round the whole camp, faster than you can chase a rat up a pump and there were plenty of rats on "The Rock", though not many pumps.

In December, orders came through that we were to embark on board a ship and sail that night under the cloak of darkness. A bright spark amongst us, who boasted a black belt in the Kama Sutra, had already worked out when we woke up in the morning, if we were sailing into the sun, then we were on our way to North Africa, but if the sun was behind us, we were going home. No chance. When we opened our eyes, the next morning, the sun was off the port bow. (See how nautical I've become in only one paragraph – "port bow".) Alas, we were heading for North Africa, on our way to relieve the 4th British Division.

We disembarked at Port Taufiq, somewhere near Cairo and marched, full kit, a few miles inland, where we set up camp and, in real earnest, ran around hiding in, under and between sand dunes and jumping in and out of the Sweet Water Canal. If you weren't very careful you could finish up with a bayonet up your London Derry Air.

The sergeant used to say to us "When the enemy is in your sights you keep firing at him even if you run out of bullets."

Not that it bothered me, I was a stretcher bearer and didn't have a gun. One thing did bother me though. I knew I was a stretcher bearer, my mates knew I was a stretcher bearer but I wasn't sure if the Germans and Italians knew that I was a stretcher bearer and they were firing the bullets coming towards me.

Then "Luck" popped its head up again for me. This time arriving in the shape of Harry Roy's Band. In a bid to boost the troops' moral before our C.O. had his long awaited want fulfilled, by having a go at the Boche.

Harry Roy had a bunch of great musicians a really swinging band. In particular we all loved the blonde singer.

Then Harry Roy started to introduce a novelty number. He wanted a soldier to come up and conduct the band. Usually, during the course of this, the band would play either too fast or too slow, having great fun at the novice conductor's inability to keep time.

As an old pro' of at least six years, I was a bit reluctant to get up on the stage, but several of my mates started to chant, "Come on, Vaughany, get up on the stage and conduct the band. Come on, Vaughany!" etc. etc.

This chant was picked up by a few hundred others and before I knew where I was. Yes up there on the stage, not only covered in embarrassment, but by sand and flies. It was a hot night.

Harry Roy told me that the music I was to conduct was "The Sheikh of Arabia". Quick as a flash, I asked him to tell the boys to play the second chorus as a stop chorus and I would do a tap dance.

So off we went, me conducting the band and lo and behold the lads in the band didn't play around and when we got to the stop chorus I did a tap dance. There was I, an eight stone rookie, in combat gear with huge army boots, weighing nearly as much as me, bucking and winging my way through a chorus of The Sheikh of Arabia.

It brought the place down. As Eric Morecambe would have said, "The lad's never gone so well."

The next morning I was ordered to report to Divisional Headquarters.

Evidently the Regiment had a divisional concert party, a talented bunch of people. A very funny comic and a crooner who sang like Bing Crosby, but a tap dancer they didn't have and one who could dance in army boots was like discovering a gold mine. I was immediately plucked from the ranks and within twelve hours posted to the Division's concert party.

I left quickly in case they changed their minds, with Sergeant Major's last words ringing in my ears.

"You Lucky Bastard."

Lucky, I certainly was. From now on I lived the life of Riley. A bit like "It Ain't 'Alf 'Ot Mum". We were allowed to grow our hair a little longer, no short back and side. My other colleagues were actors, singers, dancers and musicians. We were at least ten miles behind the front line.

I lived like this for the next two years, whilst The Regiment fought at The Angio Beachhead, the Rapido River and Monte Casino. In those three battles alone my brigade lost nearly seventy percent of its men and went on to fight throughout Italy until reaching the German border. Yes, indeed I was a "Lucky Bastard".

IAN CARMICHAEL

The Day The Circus Came To Town

After the defeat of Germany in the second world war, I was seconded from the Armoured Brigade Headquarters with which I had served for the previous two years to the Army Welfare staff of General Brian Horrocks, 30 Corps, Headquarters. There I was to act as Staff Captain to an old friend of mine from our drama student days in '38/39, then a major who subsequently became a leading theatrical agent in London. He still is.

During the second half of '45 until my demob in July '46 we were jointly responsible for providing entertainment for army personnel then occupying an area of Germany about the size of Wales. This we did by producing a series of home-grown soldier shows, also by harnessing German talent – along with that of other displaced nationals – with which we formed several continental variety shows. It was hard work, great fun and very rewarding until the circuses entered our lives. Germany was then – and perhaps still is – a land of circuses, as we were soon to find out.

We started out with one – Circus Altoff. For it's opening fortnight we sent it to Osnabruck. On the first Wednesday morning the lady proprietor arrived in our office.

"Herr Kapitan," she started, "in Osnabruck this week is also Circus Heimsoth. Is not possible two circuses can do good business in one town. What you do for us, please?"

I apologised for the double booking but until her arrival, I explained, I had no knowledge of Circus Heimsoth's existence. Only one solution seemed possible. I got into a car and set off for Osnabruck. There I interviewed the proprietor of Circus Heimsoth and suggested that, in his own interests, maybe in future we should route his circus too, to avoid another clash. He readily agreed and in two weeks time we sent Circus Heimsoth to Hanover and Circus Altoff to Hamlin.

On arriving in the office on Tuesday morning, Effi Plotz of Circus Altoff was waiting for me once again.

"Herr Kapitan," she began dolefully, "in Hamlin this week is Circus Charlie. Is not possible two circuses can do good business in Hamlin. What you do for us, please "?

Practically before she had finished, Herr Heimsoth also arrived in the office.

"Herr Kapitan, in Hanover this week is also Circus Bruckenbeck – " etc etc etc etc.

I had little choice but to visit the circuses Charlie and Bruckenbeck and make to them the same suggestion that I had made two weeks previously to Circus Heimsoth.

By the end of six weeks we were routing eight circuses. It was a nightmare. More elephants, more horses, more sealions to feed. When I finally left Germany I prayed fervently that I should never see another circus as long as I lived.

PATRICK MOORE

The Red Baron

I was never any more than a "wartime irregular". The Armed Forces are not in my line at all. Therefore I will confine my comments to two remarks which stick in my mind even after about half a century.

At the start of the war, I volunteered as a flyer (I admit that I was under age, but no matter!), I became a navigator – or, rather, observer. However, at one stage any commissioned flyer who wasn't a pilot had a chance to take "wings" on Tiger Moths. I did so. I was a rotten pilot, as I well knew, and on one occasion my C.O. saw me landing a Moth after I had been up for a meteorological test. His comment was, "If you'd been a fighter pilot, you'd have won an Iron Cross!"

The other comment was made by my Commanding Officer after one had to memorise some orders which, for various reasons, weren't the sort that were wisely written down. I did so. Then I said, "Well, these seem fairly fool-proof"

The C.O. looked at me. "Kid", he said gloomily, "With you around, they've got to be."

He may well have been right.

BERYL REID

Hitler, Penicillin and Cherry Brandy

My war was very eventful.

In 1941, just before Christmas I was in pantomime with Jack Buchanan at Sheffield and was living in a terraced house in a street which contained 300 houses. One night the bombs came and all but three houses were destroyed. My understudy, who was living next door to me, was killed. That night I wouldn't come out of my digs for a while because I had things in there that I wanted to keep – like my wireless set and a little ring that my Mother and Father had given me for my 21st birthday. At some time during the night I was forced to leave the house because of the fires around it, but I still kept returning into the building to save as many of my precious things as I could – all my hair got burnt off as well as my eyelashes and eventually they persuaded me to leave the house at 4 a.m. I was unable to carry all my belongings so somebody volunteered to take my things to Jack Buchanan's hotel in Sheffield. I had my Christmas dinner at a communal feeding centre.

In the theatre during 1941 we played performances mornings and afternoons, but never in the evenings because of the bombing. I then did a long stint in Ensa, and during this time we all longed to get invitations to play at American camps because we knew that the Yanks stocked the best in food and drink.

At one stage, I toured with Will Fyffe, a very famous Scots comedian, and the whole ENSA troop were men with the exception of myself and the Dagenham Girl Pipers. Because I was a girl I was expected to go to the butchers in every town we played, to get the troop something to eat. In one town I succeeded in getting a huge pork pie after having the butcher pinch my bottom (I was very young in those days!). I cut the pie up and gave it to the troop who by this time were on the train waiting to take us to another town, but when eventually I got to my piece of pie I saw that it was full of black mould inside.

The men were all playing cards in a reserved compartment of the train whilst I wasn't so lucky and had to stay in the corridor of the train. I had shoes with wooden soles as you couldn't get any decent shoes at this time. These wooden shoes, almost clog like, were very wearable, and your feet didn't get tired. I waited for all the men to die after eating this mouldy pie – I didn't tell them and just put mine under the seat. As it turned out the pie didn't do anyone any harm at all – perhaps this was the beginning of penicillin.

I used to stay in the Ensa hostels in some places and I remember that we used to walk about 4 miles to the pub in one town because this particular pub had a bottle of cherry brandy. I don't even like cherry brandy – it was just such a luxury to have something like that during the war.

DAVID TOMLINSON

Assiniboia, Goodwill Tours and Edward G. Robinson.

I had been selected for flying training and was on my way to Canada. We disembarked at Moncton, a town on the Northumberland Strait, that sliver of the Gulf of St Lawrence which separates Prince Edward Island from New Brunswick. We were soon to be transported by luxury train across the provinces of Quebec and Ontario and round the Great Lakes to Saskatchewan. It was a wonderful journey – quite unforgettable.

There, I was first stationed at Assiniboia. The nearest cities had very evocative names – Moose Jaw and Maple Creek. Assiniboia itself seemed the prototypical one-horse town. There was one main street and if the cars had been exchanged for horses they could have shot a cowboy film the authenticity of which would have made John Ford proud. However, down that main street, naturally enough, was that wonderful invention of the New World – the drugstore. There at the dining counter was the kind of food of which one only dreamed back home in those days. I sat at the drugstore counter and enjoyed the huge platter of bacon and eggs. The girl behind the counter was a bit surprised by the strange accent. She regarded me quizzically.

"Where you from?" she asked.

"London," I replied.

"London – Ontario?"

"No, London, England."

She looked at me. She was not about to be taken in.

"OK. Smarty Pants. You want some more coffee ?"

Assiniboia was where I did my elementary flying training. I found myself in a Cornell, a single engine monoplane, preparing to solo. This was always a big moment for every would-be pilot in training and by the time a trainee got the nod from his instructor he was itching to be given the go-ahead. I was no exception and as I was the only pupil on the course with a flying licence I was likely to be the first to solo.

The initial solo involves a circuit and landing of the aerodrome. This consists of taking off into the wind and, at about six hundred feet after levelling off, doing a ninety-degree crosswind turn to port, shortly turning again to port which brings the aircraft flying downwind, i.e. in the opposite direction from take-off. At the right point after two more identical turns the aircraft is in a position to land into the wind onto the runway.

My time had come and I was delighted. My instructor, Sergeant Rathbone, got out of the aircraft and told me what I longed to hear.

"Off you go," said Sgt Rathbone, having made his safety straps safe so that they could not entangle with the control column in his cockpit thereby interfering with mine.

It was an even tougher winter than usual in Canada that year. The snow was deep and the temperature fierce and bitter.

I took off and did all the right things, but on the downwind leg of my circuit I was stunned and horrified. The engine had cut out and the propeller was stock-still in front of me. By instinct I turned into wind and from then on luck was on my side. By good fortune I missed some telegraph wires and went between them and the ground. More luck allowed me to pancake the aircraft into deep snow. The aeroplane was quite undamaged.

Although I was in sight of the control tower it took the blood wagon an hour and a half to reach the aircraft and me. It seemed longer than ninety minutes as there was no cabin heat. I had switched everything off.

When they finally arrived the mechanics confirmed that the aircraft was undamaged and discovered that the engine failure was due to an air-lock in the fuel system. Subsequently my instructor flew the aircraft out after a tractor had cleared the snow to make a reasonable runway for take-off.

I was returned to base on the blood wagon and immediately found myself before the C.O. He seemed pleased with me. Aircraft were in short supply.

He took me to the tarmac and pointed at another Cornell. "Off you go, circuit and landing", he said.

I was delighted and he was still there when I returned having done just that.

"Well done," he said – and that was the end of an eventful day. For a very short time I was Assiniboia's hero.

It would have been reward enough for my six months of diligence to get my wings but there was more. We were chosen to go a goodwill tour of Canada. The first stop was Winnipeg where we were greeted as heroes – everything was done to make us comfortable. Bands played and twenty-eight pretty girls were produced to escort us. They took us, individually, home with them where their mothers put on a vast spread. They were wonderfully welcoming and did their best to make us feel part of the family. They usually succeeded.

Next came Toronto and the same again – twenty-eight girls and twenty-eight family meals.

Then Montreal. We made our way eastward back to Moncton feted at every stop. Canadian hospitality was overwhelming for some of my charges loose after hard training. At each port of call I lost some. With trepidation I (and my depleted contingent) arrived at Moncton. I went to report to the adjutant. What,

I wondered, would be my fate?

Cashiered at least.

"Oh hello," he said. "Where you from?"

"Weyburn," my voice was low.

"Jolly good. How many chaps have you got with you ?"

I tried evasion. "Well actually . . ." It was no good. Anyone could count. "They're not all here," I admitted.

"Oh well, they'll turn up. Happens all the time on these goodwill tours. Transport home's not ready yet anyway.

Transferred to Booker airfield new High Wycombe I trained young army NCO's destined for the Rhine crossing, Arnhem and, if need be, Japan. I spent the rest of the war at Booker and life there under our charming officer Wing Commander O'Donnell was delighted. Twice I was seconded to a film unit.

The first film was Journey Together, a Ministry of Information film, written by Terence Rattigan and directed by John Boulting. This was the first feature-length film (outside the USSR) to be sponsored entirely by a government. It was written, produced, photographed and acted by members of the RAF and was about the training of flying personnel – and American and British co-operation. Only three civilians appeared in it – Ronald Squire, Bessie Love and Edward G. Robinson, who arrived by bomber from the States and took no salary for his role.

I was fascinated by Robinson. Here was a tiny little man with a big stomach and a big bottom who played everything – romantic leads, intellectuals and gangsters. He had enormous sensitivity which was also reflected in his magnificent art collection. He didn't, however, have an easy family life. His wife was manic-depressive and his son also deeply disturbed. Robinson told me of the day he chopped down the front door with a hatchet. But he remained, despite it all, a charmer and a wonderful laconic story-teller.

"There was this old farmer," he told me, "sitting in a rocking chair out on the porch on a Saturday night with his wife, watching the sun going down over the prairie.

"'You know what, Martha?' the man said chewing his pipe and rocking gently.

"'What, George?'

"'Everything's great.'

"'That's right, George.'

"'Cattle are doin' great.'

"'That's right, George.'

"'Wheat's in the barn.'

"'That's right, George.'

"'Everything is fine and dandy.'

"'Fine and dandy, George.'

"'You know, Martha ,but for one thing I'd be a very happy man.'

"'What's that, George?'"

Robinson then left a very lengthy pause.

"'When I think of our daughters laying out there in the graveyard: sometimes I wish they were dead.'"

TOM FINNEY

Royal Army F.C.

On being called up for Military Service in April 1942, I was posted to Bovington Camp in the Royal Armoured Corps and passed out as a driver mechanic after initial training of four months and was posted to Catterick for further training. Then in December 1942, I was posted abroad to the Middle East and once arrived in Cairo was under canvas near the Pyramids, then posted to Abassia Barracks just outside Cairo.

Whilst there I played for a soccer team called the Wanderers FC comprising mainly service members from the Armed Forces with quite a number of professional players from Football League Clubs, i.e. Mickey Fenton (Middlesborough), Harry Clifton (Newcastle), Don Kelly (Newcastle), Willie Redpath (Motherwell) John Galloway (Glasgow Rangers) Andy McLaren (PNE), Ginger Walters (Chester City) and many more too numerous to mention, and toured Palestine and Syria with them on two occasions playing various service sides in Tel Aviv, Damascus, Jerusalem and many other well known places.

I was then transferred to Italy in 1945 to a transit camp in Bari. On arrival I was summoned to the CO's office and asked if I had seen any military action. I answered "No, Sir," and was

told I b----y soon would, and was on my way the following day to join the 9th Queens Royal Lancers and stayed with them until I came out of the forces in June 1946, having enjoyed the fellowship and comradeship of many brave and wonderful people. I came out a much wiser young man with a wealth of experience and understanding how people react under the stress and reality of war and death.

Professor R.V. Jones

Christmas Eve 1940

Thanks to our cryptographers at Bletchley, who "broke" the German Enigma machine, I was sometimes able in the Blitz to predict during the afternoon which of our cities was going to be attacked that night.

What Enigma would tell me were the directions on which the Germans intended to aim their X radio beams to guide their pathfinders, Kampf Gruppe (Bomber Group) 100, to its targets in Britain. I could therefore work out where the blow would fall, and warn our fighters, guns, and civil defences accordingly.

The afternoon of 24th December 1940, though, was different: we learned from Enigma that since it was Christmas Eve, the Luftwaffe would not be undertaking any operations, and so we would be able to enjoy our first quiet night since 7th December.

Following the example of the Luftwaffe, I was therefore about to "pack up shop" and go home when my door opened and in came Margaret Blyth looking for her husband Harold, a Flight Lieutenant who had been helping me throughout the Blitz. Normally all visitors, family or otherwise, would have been barred from my office for it was in the Top Secret Headquarters of MI6; indeed we were not even allowed to tell our families where we worked. Margaret, or "Maggie", though, was special, because she herself was a cryptographer at Bletchley and hence knew our secrets and had the freedom of our building.

She had come up to London and, her duty finished, she was trying to find Harold for their journey home. "Hello, Doc, have you seen Harold?" she asked. I told her that he was somewhere around the office and she was welcome to wait until he appeared.

"Anyway, Maggie," I said, "You can go home and sleep soundly in your bed tonight."

"Why?" she asked, and I told her that we had learnt from Enigma that the Germans were not coming out, because it was Christmas Eve.

"In that case, Doc," she said, "to hell with bed! We're going across to The Feathers (a hostelry in Broadway opposite our office) and, what's more, you are coming with us!"

On Harold's return we therefore went over to The Feathers together with a Squadron Leader colleague, John Perkins. Once we were inside the pub, which was of course "blacked out", we found the bar full of Christmas cheer, and before long Maggie said, "Come on, Doc, play us a few carols on your mouth-organ."

One carol led to another, including *Stille Nacht*, which struck me as a peculiarly appropriate tribute to our German opponents who were giving us a quiet night. Suddenly I saw Maggie whip off Harold's RAF cap and start to take a collection. John Perkins promptly followed her example and, to my embarrassment, they collected fifty-one shillings and sixpence, which was quite a sum for those days.

My embarrassment was solved by putting the money into the pub's own Spitfire Fund, but in addition John Perkins had collected a tribute that I still treasure. It came from a Londoner sitting in lone morosity at the far end of the bar, his head propped up on his hands.

He, of course, did not have the benefit of our privileged knowledge about Kampf Gruppe 100, but he had evidently been determined to have his usual Christmas drink, Luftwaffe or no Luftwaffe, Blitz or no Blitz, and by this time he had had several. Seeing the RAF cap thrust on the bar in front of him he put his hand in his pocket, pulled out a half-crown, and dropped it into the cap. In a voice laden with alcohol he asked the Squadron Leader, "Who's the chap who's playing? What does he do?"

John replied, "Oh, I don't know – he's a scientist of some sort," whereupon our benefactor put his hand into his pocket again, and dropped a second half-crown into the cap with the sad comment, "They're badly paid, poor buggers!"

In vino veritas.

ANNE SHELTON

The Lilli Marlene Girl

In 1940 at the age of twelve, I signed a contract with Ambroses' Orchestra. I also toured the army, navy, and airforce camps under "lease lend", all over the country, and was given a programme on Radio for the Armed Forces by Cecil Maddern. The programme, which was called "Calling Malta", lasted for five years, and at one time we were the only link with Malta during the whole of the siege.

At the same time, I was also given a programme called "Introducing Anne", which was beamed to the North African desert, and had the opportunity to perform with Mr Ambrose in a concert at the Queensbury Club. Here I met the Prime Minister, Winston Churchill, who told me that I had a very warm and compelling voice. My sister and I were very excited by this. A week later, I was called to the BBC, and was told that I was going to have my own series. Today that would be like getting your own television series. I was terribly thrilled about it. The show contained eight musicians, and Stanley Black, who was my pianist at the time, was the Musical Director. We all had signature tunes in those days, and I was told by Cecil Maddern that the show was going to have the German song "Lilli Marlene" as the signature tune. Stanley played it, and I said, "I don't like that, Cecil, I'd rather not do that." He countered by saying, "My dear, the reason you're getting the programme is that you are going to counteract the Nazi propaganda programme that is being put out by Goebbels by Leila Anderson. Our boys are listening to it, therefore *you* are going to counteract that programme. So I sang the tune for about twelve weeks, and then in time they bought in Tommy Connor who wrote the English lyrics. So that's how I became known as the Lilli Marlene girl.

Yet during this infamous time, I was called up by the BBC to answer a question from the War Office that a photograph of me had been discovered on a German Officer. They demanded to know how it got there. Had I any contact with this German Officer? I told them that the German must have taken it off one of our boys, as you couldn't write to the enemy, could you, during the war. And one would not want to anyway!

Our programme gradually became more popular than Leila Anderson's German propaganda programme, and even the Germans started listening to my programme. Some 40 years later I learned this to be so when I went to Winnipeg in 1980 with my husband to do a show for the RAF. There were over 3,000 airmen, and air crew present and I met Johnny Johnson, and Dennis Crowley-Milling and of course Douglas Bader. I also met Adolf Galland the great German air ace and wartime airforce leader who had been trying to knock down our boys all the time. Adolf told me that he had tuned into my Lilli Marlene during the war, and that he liked mine better than the German programme!

I remember also that I was very fortunate to do one of the very first Guinea Pig shows for Archibald McIndoe, the great skin graft surgeon, down in East Grinstead. I went into a room which was very dimly lit, and had a barrel of beer on a table.

72

People told me that they were celebrating the fact that Charlie's eyelids had taken, but I'm afraid I didn't know at the time what they were talking about. After I had sung three or four songs, I didn't get the applause that I got from other shows. It was only when the lights were turned on in the room that I realised that all the young RAF patients were in the first stage of skin grafting and had their hands wired together. A young pilot kissed me – his face was so soft. Just then one of the other chaps said, "You do realise that he has just kissed you with his bottom!"

CLIFF MICHELMORE

Match Of The Day

When war came upon us I was in France, part of the Advanced Air Striking Force, a stirring title for a far from stirring force.

We found remnants and relics of the First World War all around our dispersed airfields at Berry-au-Bac. Bits of old shell cases and helmets, rusted wire and collapsed trenches. We took over where they left off twenty one years before. For eight months we were on inactive service. We flew a few leaflet raids, the odd border patrol which made certain not to intrude into enemy air space, and a little safe bombing and gunnery practice down in the Mediterranean. It was called the period of the "Phoney War".

Just before the shooting started, a football match was arranged in Paris between the AASF and the French Air Force. We reported to a small hotel near the stadium and found the Warrant Officer waiting.

"You are all confined to this hotel. No going out. We take a look at the stadium at 15.00 hours, light training, then supper, then bed. Understand?"

That old service instruction again. We understood. Everybody did when faced with a Warrant Officer. Came the night and after

74

supper to a man we went down the fire escape and out into the streets of the sin-filled city of Paris. I ought to explain that so far in my life I had only breached my "Band of Hope Pledge" by having the occasional glass of shandy. Strong drink was not in me. That evening we sat in an *estaminet* and the drinks came strong and mixed. Starting at one end of the line of bottles we drank our way along: Cointreau, then Benedictine, Creme de Menthe, Brandy . . . It was the colour I liked. We were helped by the barmaid who, when paid with a fifty franc note, gave us change plus our fifty-franc note back.

I was the first to go back to the hotel. Next morning I woke cradling a bottle of Negretti rum in my bed but, surprisingly, I had no headache. There was also no sign of one of our players. Charlie the captain, a part-time professional with a West Country club and the centre-half, had not returned from the night's operations. The Warrant Officer demanded to know where he was. Out for a little training run. He would be back. He wasn't, and so a search party was despatched. We hailed a passing taxi which was driven by a man from Birmingham who had stayed on after "the first lot".

After describing where we had been the night before, he took us direct to the local brothel out of which Charlie was falling. We put him in the taxi. He neither knew us, not where he was, nor where he had been. It was five minutes into the first half when he was felled. Our trainer came on and douched Charlie with the sponge. The black hair shook the water away, he felt his unshaven chin and asked. "Which way are we kicking, Mitch?" and "What's the score?"

"We are one down and playing that way."

75

His rude reply shocked our trainer. His actions on the field of play shocked our French allies. He played a blinder. We won three-one and were promised medals to commemorate the event but we never got them.

After the war I met Charlie in Torquay. He was with his wife and he gave me a knowing wink and a conspiratorial smile. He had given up football and was driving a taxi. "I like taxis," he said.

SIR MATT BUSBY

On Me Head, Sarge

I was playing at Liverpool when I received my call up papers. It was National Service in those days and you just had to go. I went in to the 9th Battalion of the Kings Regiment, and I think because of my fitness was made P.E. instructor, the camaraderie was great and of course everyone wanted to play football: it got you out of peeling the spuds!

LORD BRIAN RIX

The Honoured Guest

I joined the Royal Air Force on Saturday 22nd July 1944 with a suitable theatrical flourish. My sister Sheila, a WAAF officer, had a Free French Major in tow. It was just before he went back to France to continue the fight on his own soil – but he was very keen on Sheila and very keen to impress all the family that his feelings were genuine. Once he got back to France that keenness rapidly evaporated, but on Saturday 22nd July 1944 he was still on the boil and volunteered to drive me to Scarborough some thirty-odd miles from Hornsea.

So there I was in a dirty great Staff Car – chauffeured by a Free French Major, with a WAAF Section Officer riding shotgun. I sat at the back in regal, if somewhat car-sick, splendour.

We duly arrived outside the Prince of Wales Hotel, Scarborough, where 34 Flight E Squadron, No 36 R & C Wing was stationed. A squad of men was drilling smartly on the promenade outside. Their instructor saw our Staff Car slowing to a halt, two officers in front, and began to wonder nervously who on earth was in the back. The rear offside door opened. Corporal Collinson (for such was the Corporal's name) decided discretion was the better part of valour, called his men to a heel – stamping attention and brought up the most tremendous salute. Out of the car stepped 1559333 AC2 Rix B.N.R. and politely enquired from the Corporal where the guard room was. Much suppressed laughter in the ranks and the Corporal told the new recruit, in no uncertain terms, where he could find the bloody place. Actually, he was a splendid chap and we became good friends even though he was the Drill Instructor for our flight.

The motley collection of new arrivals settled themselves, uncertainly, on the appointed benches and waited for all the horrible things that were going to happen to us. They did – but not before I saw someone else with long hair sitting beside me. Long hair, in those days, denoted you were " arty" so I en-quired if he was an actor. He turned out to be a pianist called Tommy Watt – newly departed from the superb Carl Barriteau band. We have remained friends every since but then we were more preoccupied with the horrors of our first R A F haircut. It was just as ghastly as we had expected, and even in July the wind whistled round our shaven necks. All the other delights came, too, in rapid succession. Kit issue and those lovely boots that not only blistered your feet but also blistered your ankles and shins as well. Buttons that had to be polished and polished – I wish I'd had shares in Duraglit – and vests and underpants I used to great comic effect when I finally returned to civvy street.

One compensation. Because we were potential aircrew, we wore little white flashes at the front of our fore and aft caps. This gave us a great feeling of superiority over lesser mortals – although not one of our bunch ever qualified as a pilot. The war ended before we were needed, so everyone was made redundant. Even in those days, that ghastly word was in common usage.

LESLIE THOMAS

The Sting

It was the King's Birthday Parade on the Padang in Singapore, with the temperature in the 90's and our Pay Corps unit left standing for more than an hour. The inspecting officer was Field Marshal Sir John Harding GOC Malaysia and, as he eventually reached our unit and we presented arms, a wasp settled on my nose and proceeded to climb up my nostril. Had I been a guardsman I would probably have fainted, but we don't do that sort of thing in the Pay Corps. Sir John noticed the back legs of the wasp kicking from my nostril and took a pace closer. As he did so the wasp flew away.

"Good God!" he said before moving on.

Years later I met him personally and although he did not remember me, he remembered the incident – and the wasp!

MICHAEL DENISON

The Intelligence Officer

My posting to the Intelligence Corps depot at Oriel College, Oxford, marked the beginning of the second and longest of the three periods of my army career. It was to last four years until the summer of 1945.

Without, I hope, endangering myself under the Official Secrets Act, I can reveal that military intelligence divides itself into two main activities: finding out about the enemy, then known as 1 (a); and preventing him from finding out about you, 1 (b). As a linguist, however corroded my German, I was to be trained in 1 (a), and began a long and detailed study of the German armed forces, and the Geneva Convention designed to make me – after some linguistic brushing up – into an interrogator of enemy prisoners. Courses at Oxford and Matlock paved the way, and then I was despatched for some practical experience of working with troops, on attachment to 59 Reconnaissance Battalion in Northern Ireland. The letter telling me who and where they were, I was ordered to memorise and destroy. I was convinced that on the long journey to Ulster I was bound to forget the contents – an essentially civilian nightmare, but fortunately with a happy ending.

Ballykinler Camp was, and no doubt still is, a scattering of bleak huts among sand dunes on the coast of County Down within sight of the Mourne Mountains. I was installed in the office of Lieutenant Abbots, the battalion intelligence and entertainment's officer, a cheerful bucolic person, nicknamed "Crash" because of certain adventures with a motor-bike, with whom I struck up a firm and still enduring friendship. It was a good partnership; I knew more, academically, about the German army and about entertainment's, and he had the practical know-how which made the most of our joint gifts in the desert of Ballykinler.

My next move, and my first actual appointment, was to join the Intelligence staff at H.Q. British troops in Northern Ireland at Lisburn near Belfast.

Early in 1942 there came the Americans. Liaison with them provided many surprises and welcome breaks in office routine, and exposed many misconceptions on both sides. I, for instance, expected swift-moving, wise-cracking men of action. But their divisional intelligence chief, a colonel of cavalry who was the first we met, belied all this. He was tanned and very handsome, with piercing blue eyes and fair, crinkly hair; he wore beautifully cut breeches and highly polished boots and – a great innovation to us – he displayed his colonel's insignia and medal ribbons on his shirt. He was utterly charming, but had a great problem understanding us, and after almost every sentence he would say "Check". It was some time before we understood that this meant "Please, say that again." Conversation proceeded slowly.

Some weeks after his arrival we received from him a communication in so many envelopes marked Top Secret that we fully expected to be told to destroy it before reading. It turned out to be a request for the rate of flow of all the German rivers.

This, remember, was some three years before the Allies were to see a German river, so the gallant colonel clearly believed in being prepared. Perhaps he needed the intervening time to digest the information, which as I remember we found in the Lisburn public library, but of course despatched to him in as many envelopes as protocol demanded.

We had one German army uniform in Northern Ireland and I was sent round with it on a tailor's dummy to demonstrate it with various badges of rank to the American troops. I gave two or three shows in the mornings and after lunch was asked to test those in each unit who claimed to speak German. The first list filled me with trepidation – Holzheimer, Muller, Vorster etceteras. Surely they should be testing me ? But no, they were mostly third generation immigrants whose grandparents were wholly German-speaking but whose parents were already bi-lingual.

At one unit I was honoured by an invitation to lunch with the colonel. He said immediately that he would very much like my opinion on some whiskey which he had bought locally. I was only too happy to oblige, until the first sip exploded at the back of my mouth and pursued its downward path like a stream of fire. The colonel was watching me closely.

"Yeah," he said on seeing me wince. "You see what I mean? It's watered."

Some months later I wore that uniform, as a German prisoner being interrogated, at a demonstration of a divisional HQ in the field, which had been arranged for the king who was on a tour of inspection.

The divisional intelligence officer and I prepared about five minutes of question and answer in German, and waited for a tip-

84

off that the royal party was approaching. The signal came and we started off. I was very aware of the king standing beside me, and also that he was showing no sign of moving on and that we were rapidly running out of prepared dialogue. We were just starting to improvise when he moved away. A moment later he was back, catching my interrogator and me shaking hands.

"Do you get much chance to speak German?" he asked.

"Not much so far, sir," I replied.

"Nor do I," he said. "But I was surprised to find how much I understood of what you were saying. Of course," he added, "we all spoke German as children."

HARRY CARPENTER

Knockout Code

I served in the Royal Navy as a wireless telegraphist. I was a Morse Code tapper. I think they call them radio operators today, if Morse Code still exists.

In 1944 I switched from the routine business of dots and dashes and became a sub-hunter, known as an " S" rating. It was all a bit hush-hush in those days.

We were listening for German U-boats. Submarines had to make the occasional signal to base, letting them know when they would be back and what supplies they would need for the next operation.

Understandably, U-boats did not want to hang around on the surface too long and less still did they want to make lengthy radio signals which could be detected and traced.

U-boats, therefore, sent extremely short encoded messages, prefaced by what was known in the trade as B-bar, i.e., dah-dit-dit-dit-dah.

The B-bar was transmitted very slowly and was quite dramatic in its effect, particularly on those who were listening for it, like us.

When you heard a B-bar you had to get your HFDF (high

86

frequency direction finding) set locked on to the signal and, with any luck, get a bearing on it. You had about 15 seconds – no more to do the trick.

If one or more other " S" ratings around the Mediterranean, where I was stationed, also heard it and got the HFDF set on to it, you had a cross-bearing and, bingo, you knew where the U-boat was lurking.

Exciting stuff. So I'm told.

I never heard a B-bar.

I suppose you could call me a B-bar black sheep.

CLIVE DUNN

Army Logic

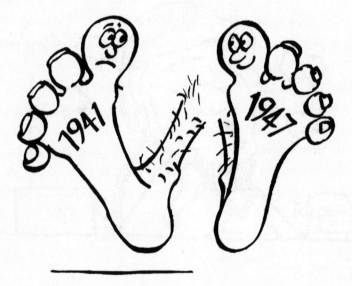

When I joined the army in May 1941 my medical report said: "Flat feet will improve with army training." When I was demobbed in 1947 my last medical reported: "Flat feet will improve with civilian living."

MICHAEL BENTINE

The Long Dark Night

Michael Bentine joined the RAF and eventually became an Intelligence Officer. He was posted to the Bomber Station at Wickenby, an it is here that this story unfolds.

I lost one friend during my time at Wickenby, and saw him in clear moonlight within hours of his passing.

Flight-Lieutenant W. was referred to as "Pop" because he was in his mid-thirties. A large, affable northerner with a sound, serious streak, he often dropped into our Intelligence operations room to discuss whatever 'gen' we could give him about the latest developments in the air war. We often chatted about the paranormal. He was sceptical but, being an open-minded and fair man, also interested in the subject.

My SIO, whom we all like enormously, had told me to take a forty-eight hour pass, which he knew I needed to go down to London and see my small family. My marriage was going badly, and I wanted to see them, so I took his advice and, before I left, my navigator friend came over to say good-bye.

He had just finished his first tour of thirty operations and was off on leave to see his family, which, I believe, consisted of a wife and two children.

He told me how relieved he was to have made it through the tour, and that he felt that he was in for a cushy time training other navigators for the next six months.

I was glad that he had made it and wished him well.

"Hope to see you sometime, Mike," he said, and I hurried off to get my transport to London.

It was midwinter, and the snow had fallen heavily enough to cover our dispersal quarters among the plantations of pine trees when I returned, at the usual 23.50 hours on the last night of my pass and, after reporting my return to the Guard Room, walked through the crunching layer of snow towards my hut. The moonlight was bright and near the full moon, so that when it came out from behind the scattered clouds the whole scene lit up in clear silvery light. As I approached the hut that I shared with air crew I saw the tall moustachioed figure of Flight-Lieutenant W. coming towards me.

I 'waved' a salute in greeting, and shouted out, "Hi, Pop!"

He seemed to acknowledge my presence, but continued to cross my path about ten to fifteen yards away and disappeared in the direction of his own Nissen hut opposite.

Nothing seemed unusual except that I felt a sudden chill behind another cloud and I gratefully crept into my own Nissen hut, as quietly as possible so as not to wake my sleeping friends; for they, of all of us, needed their rest. I undressed in the black-out hut by the subdued light of my torch and slipped into bed to fall asleep within minutes with the warmth of the pot-bellied stove which was still glowing dimly.

In the morning, at 6.30, I was awakened by our shared batman – a nice cheery, cockney LAC (Leading Aircraftman) who brought us our tea and shaving water.

'There's a flap on, sir,' he said. That meant the "Y" form (the teleprinted secret plan for an operation) must have come in early, "Have a nice forty-eight?"

'Not bad!' I said, sipping my 'Rosie Lee', which was so strong that the spoon nearly stood up in it.

'Bloody shame about Mr W.,' he said, sadly. 'Nice bloke – finished his tour and all. Bloody bad luck, sir!'

I sat bolt upright. 'What do you mean? I saw him last night!'

'You couldn't have, sir,' my surprised batman insisted. 'He was dead long before then!'

'When? Where? How?' I was flustered, and showed it.

'Course, you wouldn't have know, sir,' he apologised.

'He bought it with a Sprog crew what came in the day you left on your forty-eight.'

'Why?' I asked foolishly. 'He'd finished his tour. Why was he flying with a new crew?'

'Volunteered, sir, so they say. The gen is that this crew was a bit green and Mr W. agreed to show them the ropes on a night cross-country. Dunno what happened but somefink went wrong, and they pranged into the woods. Low cloud, I fink they said it was. Bloody shame! You must have been mistaken about seeing 'im, last night, sir!'

But I wasn't – I *had* seen W. within hours of his death – why I don't know.

But I *do* remember Flight-Lieutenant W., and many more like him, who had that extra something that makes all the difference between the ones who feel that it is 'Better to be a live Nazi than a dead hero' and those who, even when they were safe, still cared enough about their comrades to give them a hand.

N.B. Actually, it was a Raid on Berlin, with a *new* crew. I've just found out.

Michael Bentine 1992

JON PERTWEE

The Drill Instructor

Just how one learns to fight battles by marching round parade grounds I've never understood, but whatever service you're in, you march. We used to have to take it in turns to give commands and, when my turn came, the CPO in charge, one Chief Petty Officer Branch, said, "Right-ho, Pestwee! March that column of men to the end of the parade ground, turn 'em about, and bring 'em back 'ere in front of me."

"Aye aye, Chief," I replied confidently and gave the order, "By the left, quick march!" I waited until they'd gone some fifty yards and then shouted, "Squad, habout . . ."

"Not yet, Pestwee," said CPO Branch, "I'll tell you when." By this time they were getting out of earshot, so I shouted, with all my might, "Squad habout . . ."

"Not yet, Pestwee," said CPO Branch. I was just recovering from my last effort which had turned my face purple and caused my eyeballs to protrude, when CPO Branch said, "Right lad, now!" Rallying what little vocal resource I had left, I screamed, "Habout turn"! A scream that was heard by all at the back, some in the middle, but none in the front, so that they all started to go in different directions.

93

"Dearie me!" said CPO Branch. "Oh dearie, dearie me. What a very nasty mess ! Get 'em back together, lad."

Fighting to clear the mists that had formed before my eyes I breathed deeply, clenched my teeth and my gluteus, braced my feet and gave the piercing screech, "Haboouutt teherrrn!"

This time they all heard it and dutifully turned about. As you can imagine the result was chaotic. They all banged into each other, and several fell over . . . It was ghastly. There was a long pause then, in a voice broken with emotion, CPO Branch said, "Now I know what they mean when they say" Marines will advance in columns of fours and matelots in fuckin' great heaps."

ANTON ROGERS

Buzz Bombs

One outstanding memory of wartime was in 1944, when my family moved from Cambridgeshire to a large house in Chester Square, when London was being subjected to the infamous Buzz bombs. I was about eleven, and remember vividly the awfulness of those raids. As a family we made it a habit the moment the air raid warning was sounded to rush down to the cellar underneath the front steps, where the whole family (and there were eight in mine) would sit or lie on mattresses until the raid was over. As I was the smallest member of the family, I was always the one who had to sleep under the lowest step, and I remember clearly waking up in sheer terror when one of the buzz bombs exploded nearby, and hitting my head on the step.

This always seemed to cause great amusement to my sisters who thought it hysterically funny every time I did it. In retrospect, this may be the reason I was known as "Flathead" by my family. Thankfully the war ended soon after.

DONALD SINDEN

M.E.S.A.

Pronounced medically unfit for service in the Armed Forces, Donald Sinden held down two jobs during the Second World War. From 8 a.m. to 5 p.m. he worked as a joiner, and from 5.30 p.m. to 12 midnight as an actor for Charles F. Smith's company M.E.S.A.: Mobile Entertainments Southern Area. M.E.S.A was based in Brighton. Donald Sinden recounts the following episode:

We would set out for a performance in a Southdown bus from which half the seats had been removed to allow room for our scenery and furniture. On arrival the men erected the scenery and the girls made themselves responsible for the props and furnishings, because we carried no stage managers. Sound effects were produced by whoever happened to be in the wings at the time.

Our theatres and stages varied enormously in size: one night we might play in a building seating 2,000; the next in a Nissen hut capable of seating seventy with a stage ten feet square. Mostly our venues were village halls. I think I have played in more of these in Kent, Sussex, Hampshire and Surrey than any other actor. More often than not we all had to share a dressing room and I would find attractive girls on all sides removing their clothes – or most of them. At the end of the performance we had to pack everything back into the bus and return to Brighton.

After Dunkirk the whole of the South Coast was barricaded and only residents were allowed within fifteen miles of the coast. Gun emplacements had been dotted along the shore. We heard at first-hand the story of General Montgomery coming down to inspect the defences and asking a young subaltern if there were any problems: "Yes, sir," he said pointing to his map. "There are Howitzers here and here with a range of X yards, twenty-five pounders here and here with a range of Y yards and anti-tank guns here and here with a range of Z yards – this leaves a stretch of coast twenty yards long quite undefended. Suppose the Germans were to land there! – what should we do?"

"Count them as they come ashore, ring me up, tell me how many and I'll tell you what to do," replied Monty.

We took our plays to these gun emplacements and to ack-ack sites on the Sussex Downs. Never since have I known such enthusiastic reception or such audience participation. We were at one with them: from the hilarious moment in Private Lives when, shortly after Elyot has uttered the delightful Coward line "Don't quibble, Sybil," he handed her a cocktail and as she raised it to her lips a voice from the audience shouted "Don't dribble, Sybil," to the uncanny experience we had when playing Terence Rattigan's French Without Tears to an RAF audience.

The performance was going splendidly and the audience were on their toes, responding to every nuance when suddenly halfway through the second act the laughter ceased. Silence . . . What had happened? We cast questioning looks at each other. We continued with the dialogue haltingly . . . and then . . . stopped. We became aware of a concerted murmur . . . Wrrr . . . Trrr . . . Thrr . . . Frrr.

Unbeknown to us a squadron had set out from the RAF station during the afternoon. Now they were returning and the entire audience was counting them in as their ears picked up the drone of the engines . . . Five . . . Six . . . Seven . . . Thank God – on that occasion – they all returned. As the last was heard a cheer went up. We had all been facing each other for – what? – thirty minutes? The audience had never ceased looking in our direction, but were oblivious of our presence. Now we could breathe again and we continued with the scene to much laughter tinged with a certain hysteria – laughter of a quality I will probably never hear again.

RONNIE BARKER

Drama Masterclass

I was nearly ten years old when hostilities began. As soon as War was declared many masters had to leave the school, having been called up.

Only old teachers were left to cope. Due to lack of staff, it was decided that no school plays would be performed – no readings, absolutely no drama at all.

I've often thought that the complete freedom from the drudgery of having to sit and listen interminably to one's school fellows droning on in a hopefully inept attempt at speaking Shakespeare's blank verse must have contributed greatly to my eventual love of the Theatre.

Sir Harry Secombe

Fusilier Brown

There is one entry for January in my diary for 1943:

"Friday, 1st January: Broke my glasses on way to Green Hill."

Behind this brief sentence lies a story.

We were ordered up to the northern sector to support the Buffs of 36th Brigade in an attempt to take Green Hill, a dominating position ten miles short of Mateur. I know this now because I read it later on in the official history of the 78th Division. At the time I was only aware that I had to ride the dreaded MC 13, which was now a Matchless, 350cc, the Norton having been left behind somewhere in Tebourba. The mud was so bad that every few miles I had to undo the butterfly screws on the back mudguard and scoop out the liquid glue that clogged the wheel. Then I lost one of the screws in the stuff, and finally finding it after nearly a half-hour of searching, I kicked the starter so savagely that my glasses flew off and shattered on the petrol tank.

I managed to make the rendezvous but my eyesight was so

bad without my spectacles that I was useless for any duties other than carrying ammunition boxes and peeling spuds in the cookhouse. The attack failed – and we withdrew to positions near Medjez. Here it was decided that I was going to be a liability until I had a new pair of glasses, and I was duly sent off to the rear to get them.

For some reason I was officially classified as a "walking wounded" and put on the ambulance train to Souk Ahras, back over the border in Algeria. I was issued with a brown label with my name, rank and number on it and told to report to the General Hospital. The journey back to base was very embarrassing because there were infantrymen with bullet and shrapnel wounds sharing the same compartment. I could not bear to tell them what was wrong with me, so I cultivated an air of mystery about myself, hinting at some obscure disease.

We arrived at Souk Ahras at night time in the middle of an air raid, and things were pretty chaotic at the hospital. Those of us who could walk, shuffled in a line before a desk where our labels were taken from us. Then we sat around for a while as the bombs fell. When the all-clear went, an orderly summoned me, gave me a pair of pyjamas and told me to undress. I was in no position to question his orders, indeed I welcomed the chance of a kip in a real bed. "This is the way the British Army looks after its lads," I thought admiringly as I pulled the blankets over my head.

My memory of the next few hours is hazy – I know I was awakened and given something to drink, and remember nothing more until I was shaken awake by a doctor in a white coat.

"How are you now, Brown?" he asked.

"Pardon, sir?" I tried to bring him into sharper focus by narrowing my eyes.

He repeated the question.

"My name is Secombe, sir. Lance-Bombardier 924378." I knew that much.

The doctor looked at something tied to the foot of the bed.

"Aren't you Fusilier Brown?"

"No, sir."

"Have you got dysentery, then? The doctor was getting irritable by this time.

"No sir, I've broken my glasses," I stammered.

"Get out of that bloody bed, man." The M.O. was furious.

"Give him his uniform and send the bugger to the optician," he said to the orderly with him.

As I dressed I learned that there had been a monumental mistake and that some poor fusilier had been up all night filling sandbags in between rushing to the latrines. Then, to cap it all, he'd been given an eye test, which must have seemed a strange treatment for what ailed him.

I was given pretty short shrift, and was provided with two new pairs of spectacles in no time at all. Secretly I had banked on having to wait a couple of days while they tried to fix me up with the strong lenses I required, but had to be content with just one night's bed and board. I don't know what was in the drink they gave me that night but it was nearly a week before I had a bowel movement – and it took a mortar attack to move me.

Brian Johnston

Down in Dorset with the Guards.

I was sent on an MT course at Minehead, with a view to becoming the Transport Officer, although I was not the least technically minded. But I had a bit of luck.

At the end of the course there was to be an exam which I was dreading. On the night before, a friend who had been on the course with me was duty officer, and to his surprise found next day's questions in the in-tray in the Adjutant's room. When he came off duty he rushed round to me with a copy and we hurriedly looked up the answers. As a result I passed with flying colours, though ironically my friend only just passed.

On returning to the Battalion I was congratulated on my report and became the Transport Officer. It was a good job to have. We were left very much to ourselves, as everyone else knew even less about it than I did. I had a small élite staff of fitters and storemen and was never short of volunteers since we escaped most of the "bull" and drill parades.

It was about this time that I indulged in my habit of giving people nicknames. In a most unguardsmanlike way I gave people on my staff such names as Honest Joe, Burglar Bill, Gandhi, the Admiral, and even extended it to the officers' mess where the

Mess Sergeant became Uncle Tom.

Uncle Tom was a lovely person and looked after us superbly. He had been a cook and made the best chocolate pudding I have ever tasted. I even indoctrinated the regular officers so that in no time one could hear the Commanding Officer saying, "Another pink gin please, Uncle Tom." Scarcely credible really, when you consider the traditional discipline of the Brigade of Guards. I was especially pleased with my nickname for one of my fellow officers called Neville Berry. He was known as The Hatchet. Got it ?

Our Headquarter Company was stationed in an evacuated girls' school and some of the guardsmen slept in one of the old dormitories. They were delighted to find a notice on the wall which read: "Please ring this bell if a mistress is required during the night."

We had three visits which I especially remember. The first was from Harry Hopkins, Presidents Roosevelt's special envoy who was flying back to America from Hurn Airport after a visit to Mr Churchill. He stayed the night in our mess and breakfasted with us on powdered eggs. He was a quiet, friendly man, who looked pale and sick. He quizzed us about living conditions in Britain, and showed special interest in our families and their reaction to the bombing and blackout, obviously for the benefit of his master.

The next visit was from the Press who descended on us in a public relations exercise organised by the Army. The idea was for them to see how a Battalion worked, so when they came to me I decided to give them good value. I gave a lot of pennies to one of my clerks and sent him out to ring my office every few minutes from a call-box. While I was being interviewed by the

Press my telephone hardly stopped ringing and as a result I got a jolly good "press" the next day saying how hard an MT officer had to work.

Our most important visit at Parkstone was from Monty – he came to inspect the Battalion. We had good warning and we prepared what we thought would be an interesting display when he visited our work-shops.

We had an engine in the process of being taken out of a truck, we took a wheel off one vehicle and jacked up another, with a mechanic lying underneath it.

When Monty arrived I saluted and offered to show him round. But he would have none of it and hardly looked at our display. Instead he walked straight up to one of the trucks parked near by and asked the driver to switch on his side-lights. The driver went to his cab and turned the switch. But no lights came on. Monty went to the next truck and asked the driver to do the same thing. Again, no lights.

To my horror, this happened twice more and Monty in triumph asked one of the drivers why none of the lights came on. I was as eager to hear the answer as he was. The driver explained that a lot of bulbs had been pinched out of parked vehicles so that now whenever they left their vehicles they used to put the bulbs in their pockets. Monty had obviously been tipped off about this habit and wanted to put a stop to it. He told me what a bad habit it was as if there was an emergency and the driver was in a cinema or somewhere, his vehicle would have no lights if someone else was ordered to drive it.

I thought I had better not make things worse by telling him that the vehicles probably would not start anyway. The reason for this was that the drivers used to immobilise them by removing the rotor arms from the distributors and putting them in their pockets too.

I remember too that at lunch Monty pointedly quizzed our Commanding Officer, Lt- Col Mike Venables-Llewelyn, on how the weekly five-mile run was going. This was Monty's keep fit campaign in which everyone in the division from the highest-ranking officers to the lowest other ranks were required to go for a five-mile run once every week. Monty must have asked the question with his tongue in his cheek as Mike had what you might politely call an ample figure and could not have run one mile let alone five. He got away with it but I must admit that not many of us ever did carry out the order.

We used to set out from the mess at a trot looking very businesslike in shorts and gym shoes. But once round the corner out of sight we used to go for a walk round the block and sneak back to the mess through the back door. There was not much danger of being found out. The only risk was that one might run into Mike doing the same thing.

RICHARD WILSON

A Memory from Singapore

I was in the Royal Army Medical Corps and was eventually posted to Singapore. The abiding memory I have of Singapore is of being thrust into the middle of a multi-racial society. In the British Military Hospital we had patients from every possible Asian and African community – the Africans being part of the African Rifle Brigade, which was stationed there. I also remember the nursery was full of babies of every possible colour from deepest black to whitest white.

It was very harmonious community, and I have always cherished friends I made there amongst the Malaysians, the Chinese, the Indians and the Africans, and of course, the Brits. It was a very happy time, and I often remember the international mix in these days of small-minded nationalism.

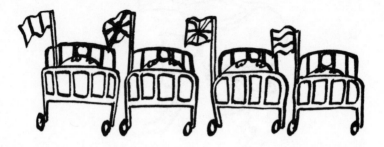

DEREK JAMESON

What Am I Doing Here?

It's 1949 and I'm doing my National Service – S/22172890 Jameson. D . . . Pte. A private in the Royal Army Service Corps. You can't get much lower than that!

Army life in earnest begins in an induction centre at North Camp, Aldershot, where we are confined to barracks for fourteen of the longest days of our lives. Beguiled, browbeaten, brainwashed into something that bears passing resemblance to a soldier. Hour after hour every day on the drill square, learning how to look the part.

Attention! Stand still, that man. Don't move a muscle. Arms tight to sides, thumbs against trouser seams, stomach in, chest out. Stand at ease, blessed relief, legs twelve inches apart, arms behind back, palms entwined. Stand easy, move, talk, scratch your bum, but keep those feet still and no smoking. Quick march, thirty-six paces a minute, fingers curled with thumb on top, swing arms shoulders high, chest out, chin in. Salute, everything that moves, palm flat, right arm longest way up to forehead, shortest way down. Plus all the variations. Jogging at the double, the funereal slow march. How to right turn, left turn and about turn. PT 6.30 every morning, games Wednesday afternoons. Rifle drill and weapon training would come later.

Our instructors are regulars, drill sergeants from the Brigade of Guards and other top regiments. All of them have been through the war and bedazzle us with the campaign ribbons on their chests. Real soldiers teaching a bunch of young, unruly civilians how to walk tall.

They also play mother and father to lads who have never been away from home and don't know how to peel a spud or make a bed.

We are introduced to foul muck called blanco, a clay-like substance that has to be dampened and made into a paste to smooth on every surface of our webbing equipment. In training that means the whole shebang every evening. Large and small packs with straps and ammunition pouched and the belt and ankle gaiters worn at all times.

On top of that little lot we burnish every brass button, badge and clasp and bull up two pairs of boots until the toecaps are mirror-bright. Knife-edge creases have somehow to appear like magic in our heavy serge uniforms. To the uninitiated, these daily chores take two or three hours. Every morning all kit is laid out on the bed in perfect symmetry for inspection. Right down to the last neatly squared sock, everything had its official place in a tableau that probably goes back to Wellington. Blankets and sheets are folded into a sandwich on the palliasse, the webbing equipment draped around it. God help anyone who presents a blanket half-inch wider than its neighbour. This is regarded as tantamount to mutiny. Reveille at 6.00. One minute the sleep of the dead after all that work and exercise, then total madness as the orderly corporal descends hollering, banging the iron bed frames, ripping off covers and threatening dire penalties for those who refuse to stir.

"Feet on the floor, feet on the floor. C'mon, let's be having you. Move, move MOVE. Anyone still in bed on the count of five is for it. One, two, three, four, FIVE!" By then even the most comatose managed one foot on the floor.

Then, the bleakest moment of all. Thirty half-asleep, irritable recruits struggling to get to one of four decrepit basins for a wash and shave in cold water in time to be on parade for physical jerks at 6.30. Breakfast at 7.00, then a mad scramble back to the barrack room to get kit laid out and please God the bastards don't poke their nose into brasses left untouched the night before.

"Stand by your beds!" comes the order from the lance-corporal who traditionally occupies the end bed. We stand there, butterflies gnawing at our stomachs, as the orderly officer and sergeant of the day enter briskly on their rounds, eager to find transgressors. The officers we hate most of all. They are second lieutenants, conscripts like ourselves, obviously selected for a commission on the basis of accent and class. In those days, any officer of working class origin must have developed a cut glass accent at grammar school. Perhaps sensing our hostility, the National Service officers treat us like dirt.

"Sergeant, this man is a disgrace," they would drawl in the languid manner adopted by subalterns. "Put him on a charge for dirty kit".

As often as not, he would poke his swagger stick into his victims pile of bedding and tip over the lot so that everything is sent flying on to the highly polished floor. We stand there, rigid, burning with anger, unable to flicker an eyelid by way of protest, while some poor sod just one week removed from his mother's loving care is treated, like a child molester because Blanco has smudged his brass.

" Sir!" roars the duty sergeant, reaching for notebook in tunic pocket.

He will take the man's name, have him listed on Company orders for an offence under Section 40 of the Army Act, in that whilst on active service he did fail properly to maintain his kit, and the commanding officer of his adjutant will dole out seven days' fatigues, known as jankers. That means reporting to the Guardroom for a week of hard labour. Extra drill, cookhouse duty, scrubbing floors, heaving coal..

He will stagger back to his barrack room every night at 1.30, time for lights out, and clean his kit in the washroom by the light shining through the window from the street lamps outside. If he is lucky, his closest mate will have done it for him.

There is no justice about it. In theory, you can appeal all the way up to the colonel commanding the battalion, but only a fool would try to buck a system going back centuries. For it is quaint old customs like these that make the British the greatest soldiers in the world. The psychology is simple. Do as you are told, do not answer back, and you will survive. Probably have a few laughs, too.

It works a treat. If a tough coalminer from Durham is prepared to put up with some wally from Surbiton with a pip on his shoulder spreading his kit all over the deck, then he'll accept anything. Anyway, that second Louis probably had it even worse when he was in training. Shot or shell, desert or snow, hell or high water, the British soldier simply gets on with it. That's what discipline is all about.

A perfect example is Morris Bennett, my managing editor when I was running the *Daily Express*. Morris won the Military

Cross as an infantry captain in Italy during the war. He fought the battle of Long Stop Hill, commanding a badly battered company that held up two crack German divisions at a narrow pass for several days in 1944.

Morris doesn't talk about it much. He was badly wounded at the time. Exercising my editor's prerogative, one day I insisted on knowing why he had dared take on Hitler's Panzer Corps against such fearful odds.

"Well, we were told to stay there, so we stayed," he said. "To be perfectly honest, I was a bloody sight more terrified of my colonel than I was of the Germans."

That's the British Army. Magnificent.

PADDY ASHDOWN

Who Needs Enemies?

I have always been fascinated by the macabre sense of humour of the average British serviceman. Even in the most difficult of circumstances, they always seem able to make a joke about danger.

When I was doing my training for the Special Boat Section, we used to do a lot of dive training in the waters around a very beautiful island off the east coast of Malaya. We were, at the time, practising diving on pure oxygen, which has the advantage of not sending bubbles to the surface, enabling clandestine work. The disadvantage, however, is that you cannot go deeper than about 30 feet without the risk of oxygen poisoning.

The waters around this island were perfectly clear and very beautiful.

However, this was an established and well known breeding ground for sharks. In fact, in the whole history of the area, for some reason, no shark had ever attacked a human being. Nevertheless, seeing a shark at close quarters when you are lumbering around with a diving set on is rather a frightening experience. They move so fast and are so agile whereas you are so slow and cumbersome. So seeing a shark (and we nearly always did with every dive) always set the heart beating a little faster.

One day I was diving with a young marine. We had dived together before. Just before we went in, we were checking each other's equipment when I noticed that he was carrying a sharp stick.

I said to him, "What's that for?"

He replied, "It's my shark stick, Sir."

I said, "Don't be silly, you'll never keep a shark off with that."

His reply was, "Oh no, Sir, that's not to keep the shark off, it's to poke you to make you bleed so I've got time to get away!"

He was, of course, joking – I hope.

Spike Milligan

Thursday, November 11th 1943.
Armistice Day. Ha Ha Ha.

Lt "Johnny" Walker is at an Op on Monte Croce. He is suspicious that a white farmhouse is harbouring the enemy, so he drops a few 200 pounders around it: as they get closer a door bursts open and out rush a Jerry patrol who run like hell to a farmhouse a hundred yards away.

Walker then shells that place, out runs Jerry back to farmhouse one, he does this till the Jerries are shagged out and finally doubleback to their own lines. "When I fight an enemy, I like to keep them fit," says Walker.

That night fairly quiet in the Command Post, Lt Stewart Pride not feeling very well. "I must report sick in the morning," he says. "Any music on the wireless?"

I fiddle with the knobs. We are surrounded by hills and the reception is very bad. I get what sounds like someone singing in Yugoslavian.

"I don't understand, Milligan," says Stewart Pride, "you can't get our bloody OP, which is only half a mile away, yet you can get some idiot singing in Yugoslavia."

"That's because he's singing very loud, sir. If our signallers at the OP could be given training in opera, it would be easy."

It's two in the morning, bloody cold. Edgington has just come off Telephone Exchange duty, he comes into the Command Post for a warm.

"Cor, it's tatters," he says, making straight for the brazier. We all stand round it, the twigs crackling.

"What was the news tonight?" says Edgington.

"The Russians are advancing in all directions including upwards. The Allies are making steady progress, and Harry Roy is in hospital with appendicitis".

Edgington grins at Stewart Pride. "Do you like Harry Roy?" he says.

"I don't know I've never met him," says Steward Pride.

Buttoning up his overcoat Edgington bids us goodnight.

"I will see 'ee in dawn's rosy light," and he slips under the canvas into the night.

We hear him fall in the dark and fade away swearing to himself. I shout through the canvas. "Don't forget, dawn's early light". Came the answer, "Balls." Oh what a lovely war. Not so lovely when we hear by the grapevine that our PBI are suffering 50 per cent casualties.

Thank God I'm not in the Infantry. So ended Armistice Day, what a day to die.

RICHARD TODD

Pegasus Bridge

Richard Todd was an officer with the Seventh Battalion of the Parachute regiment – the unit entrusted with capturing and holding Pegasus Bridge in Normandy on D. Day 1944. Here he describes the successful final stage of the operation.

All day our numbers had been swelled by men who got back to us from the scattered night-drop, some of them having found their way through enemy lines. One Sergeant-Major was led to the bridges by a French girl. She was dressed in her brother's civilian clothes and riding her brother's bike, and the pair of them had cycled some miles through German-occupied territory. By the end of the day we mustered about two hundred and fifty men, having lost some sixty killed and wounded from the original hundred and fifty that had established the bridgehead.

At around 2100 hours two marvellous moments arrived almost simultaneously. First, the leading troops of 3rd British Division reached us and immediately set about relieving the pressure on " A" and " C" Companies.

Then the sky was darkened by the arrival of two hundred and forty-five huge gliders and their tug aircraft. Within minutes two battalions of 6th Airlanding Brigade were on the ground, plus more guns. Some landed on our L.Z.* West of the Canal, but the majority flew into our dormer D.Z.* North of Ranville. It was a heart-warming sight.

Many of the tug aircraft continued towards Caen after releasing their gliders and before turning for home, obviously unaware that they were overflying ground still in enemy hands. It was sickening to see some of them shot down.

The mopping-up operation by the infantry in the Benouville area took some time, and it was midnight before our two companies were extricated from their doggedly-held positions, and the casualties evacuated.

---

* *Landing Zone*
* *Drop Zone*

By 12.30 a.m. we assembled as a battalion on the road by the Canal Bridge, and began our march to an area just North of Ranville, where we were to go into Brigade reserve.

The Gondree family was there smiling and waving as the men passed by. All day they had helped to tend the wounded who had been brought to their house after the R.A.P. had been overrun. 7th Para. Bn and the "Ox and Bucks" Light Infantry owed a great debt of gratitude to these kindly, brave people.

Already fastened to the girders of the Canal bridge was a crudely-painted sign: "PEGASUS BRIDGE", a name derived from the badge worn by British Airborne forces, the Winged Horse of Mythology. Twenty-four hours after we first set foot on that bridge, we were retracing our steps; tired, dirty, and elated. It had been a day to remember.

GEORGE MELLY

The Reason I Joined the Navy

I was sitting, less than a month off my eighteenth birthday, on the lavatory of the "green bathroom" in my parents' large comfortable ugly house in the Victorian suburbs of Liverpool, and I was crying bitterly.

The reason I was crying was because I'd just read a letter from a man called A.B. Clifford who was a house master at Stowe, the school I'd just left, and more relevantly in this context, Officer in Charge of the JTC there.

JTC stood for Junior Training Corps. When I'd arrived at Stowe, about a year after the beginning of the war, it was still called the OTC, but this had been changed to meet the democratic temper of the times. Officers Training Corps had suggested rather too blatantly that all public school boys were automatically officer material.

Changing an initial didn't mean changing anything else though. The ancient drill sergeant still called us "sir", and we dressed up every Tuesday afternoon in 1914 uniforms with puttees and brass buttons. In the summer there were occasional "field days" when we charged about the drowsy Buckinghamshire countryside pretending to shoot each other, while perspiring "umpires" decided whether we were "dead" or not.

Playing these Henty-like games made it difficult at times to remember there was a real war on and that boys we'd known well had been killed in it. Like their more fortunate contemporaries most of them had done their initial training at either Oxford or Cambridge, an arrangement which assured them of a place after the duration if and when they returned. They'd usually come down during this academic interim looking carefully languid in their new Brigade of Guards' uniforms and, more often than not, enviably drunk. Then they'd be posted and a few months later we'd be told, in Chapel, that they'd been killed on active duty.

I was enough of a realist to know that if I fell it wouldn't be in a commissioned uniform. I was patently not officer material. My putties fell down, my buttons were either dull and smeary or, if halfway bright, the Duraglit had spread over the surrounding khaki. Worse, I was always losing things and indeed, during the last week of my final term when the time had come to hand in my uniform, I'd discovered that I was short of a brass-buckled belt and one boot.

Thinking myself safe because I wasn't coming back, I'd concealed the loss from the retired sergeant in the 1829 gothic armoury and left school in high spirits with several of my contemporaries, all of us definitely puffing away at Black Balkan Sobranies through the taxi window. My confidence was misplaced. The missing items were noted and reported to Major Clifford. He bothered to write to me during his holidays, not only demanding I paid for their replacement but warning me, in an icy rage, that he intended writing to my future Commanding Officer at the Navy Shore Establishment, Skegness, informing him of my perfidious carelessness and suggesting some suitable punitive action on my arrival there. Even if Major Clifford had carried out his threat it was extremely unlikely that a senior officer, in command of the entire Royal Navy intake during the major conflict at a particularly crucial moment, could have spared much time to work himself up over the loss of two items of archaic military equipment at a distant public school. Predictably, when I get to Skegness not a word was said about either belt or boot.

My choice of the Navy is also indicative of my thinking during that period. It had nothing to do with my younger brother's success as a Dartmouth cadet, nor my father's shore-based commission in the RNVR. It was for no other reason than that I found the uniform "more amusing".

STRATFORD JOHNS

Tempting Fate

I was rather young at the end of the war and having arrived in England from South Africa, I had first to get a job. This I did and promptly volunteered for the Service in Royal Navy. I particularly wanted to fly aeroplanes in the Fleet Air Arm. However, the European war was already over by this time and it was clear that they did not know what to do with those of us who wanted to join the Fleet Air Arm because Lord Mountbatten had decided to retrain RAF aircrew for Navy aircraft rather than train fresh and aircrew. So we did not really do any fighting. As a result an old battle cruiser was brought back into service to us to send the South Africans home in. One night in very heavy seas, on the journey home just off Gibraltar, I said to an old leading seaman "It's amazing the way these old deck plates heave". He replied "Shut up you bloody fool, we are probably going to sink!" so I kept quiet for the rest of the journey.

LORD DENIS HEALEY

Bombs. Swindon Station and the Liberation

I can vividly remember my earliest days in the Army when I arrived at King's Cross on my way to Woolwich Barracks, the underground was filling up with women in slacks and pinafores with their children, seeking protection against the nightly air raid. Woolwich in the last weeks of 1940 was like Dante's Purgatory, with more than a smattering of the Inferno. Damage littered the streets. The barracks of the Artillery Depot were dirty and squalid, the beds made of iron strips with greasy "biscuits" for mattresses – no sheets of course.

There was little to do by day, and we were allowed out for only an hour or so before the blackout. Nevertheless, some of the men managed quite well. One night a stick of bombs fell in the barracks and there was an early parade to discover the casualties. Several hundred were missing; they regularly spent the night out with their girlfriends, returning only for the normal parade in the morning.

At dawn the barrage balloons looked like a swarm of silver bees, fiery with light. After sunset the air raids began with warnings from the sirens like a chorus of sea beasts moaning in the fog. Then a battery of very heavy guns behind the barracks would make the walls tremble with their WHAM, WHAM, WHAM; the more distant guns sounded like slamming doors. Meanwhile the searchlights swept and intersected in the night sky.

One evening about forty of us were sitting in the canteen, when suddenly, as if at a signal, everyone flopped to the floor. The noise of falling chairs and breaking cups made me think a bomb had fallen just outside. The room looked like a Muslim prayer meeting – a mass of khaki backsides raised to heaven and heads hidden under the marble tables. Then suddenly everyone rose again to continue talking and drinking as if nothing had happened. In fact nothing had happened; it was a good example of the psychology of crowds.

I Served at the Railway Traffic Office on Swindon station for the first months of 1941, charged with a heavy responsibility for keeping the war going. I was supposed to count all the service men and women getting on every train, getting off every train, and getting off and on again. That was not easy on six platforms in the black-out.

So I made up the number getting off and on again, made an informed guess of the number getting on, and asked the ticket collector for the number getting off. After a few weeks, I discovered he was making up his figures as well. This gave me a life-long scepticism about the reliability of statistics, which served me well when I became Chancellor of the Exchequer. It also taught me never to take for granted any information I was given unless I was able to check it from another source at least once.

At the end of the War, we entered Austria. In every village banners and flags of Free Austria were hanging out. Hordes of refugees were walking down all the roads; among them were individual German soldiers who had simply decided to walk home. The ditches were full of helmets, webbing and weapons, abandoned as they tried to lighten their load.

In Klagenfurt we stayed with a platoon of the Rifle Brigade doing guard and garrison on one of the offices of the new local government. The Austrian officials were still terrified of reprisals by the SS. The young lieutenant spoke no German and had little idea what he was supposed to do; so I acted as his guide and interpreter. Going over in the dark to the local Gasthaus to brew some tea I was met by a worried Special Forces officer in a jeep; he said that there were two thousand armed Croat Ustachis milling around in the Adolf Hitler Platz, that Tito's troops were infiltrating into the south of the town, and that there might be a major battle during the night unless the Croats were disarmed – fortunately there was not.

An Austrian of the Landesregierung said he would be murdered on his way home by the SS unless I gave him an escort.

The following morning there were stream of questioners. Two Slovens afraid of Tito wanted to know if the road to Villach was free from partisans. A young Albanian asked if he could join the British Army so as to avoid partisan vengeance; he burst into tears when I told him the war was over. A German Colonel demanded to know how to evacuate his wounded. Meanwhile the town was filling up with Hungarian troops in retreat from the Russians.

That afternoon I went over a high pass into Gorizia and territory controlled by the partisans. Yugoslav forces were now in every village; there were notices and slogans in Serbian, posters of Tito, flags and triumphal arches of pine branches and flags over the entrance to every hamlet. The situation in Trieste was extremely tense, since the political future of the area had not yet been decided. West of Trieste we passed through one of Tito's divisions on the march – a band of tough, ragged men, women and boys, all armed with captured weapons or British Sten guns, a few officers on horses and senior officers in German cars, in every type of clothing – peasant rags, or uniforms from the German, Hungarian, or Italian armies, but all wearing the partisan's grey forage cap with the red star.

DAVID JACOBS

The Holiday Camp?

David Jacobs enlisted in the Royal Navy during World War II and was posted to H.M.S. Royal Arthur for nautical training. He describes his experiences:

H.M.S. Royal Arthur turned out to be a converted holiday camp, where we were lodged in cosy chalets instead of draughty barrack rooms and slept on deep, deep mattresses instead of hammocks. Three days after our arrival we each got a hammock and a thin "biscuit" to line it.

These we lashed and stowed in seamanlike fashion each morning and unrolled each night. But we still slept on the mattresses. We were also issued with uniforms at the same time, thus ending a situation that I had been finding increasingly irritating and depressing.

I never cease being amazed at the docility or perversity with which – come war, fire or famine – we sort ourselves into class groups, or float into them from force of habit. In the three days before we got our uniforms, this draft of ordinary young civilians destined to become ordinary young seamen meticulously graded itself, without any outside help or instruction, into a series of isolated cliques in strict conformity with each individual's accent, eating habits, and relative costs of suits, linen and footwear. Sports jackets in one group, flannel shirts in another; hound's tooth sniffing defensively at herringbone; handkerchief-in-sleeve-cuff drifting quietly away from handkerchief-in-breast-pocket; in the distance blue serge and no handkerchief at all. The "gentlemen" feigned unawareness of the "yobbos"; the "yoicks" glared under their eyebrows at the "toffs". And they say it is women who are clothes-conscious!

I do not suggest it was either the "toffs" or the "yobbos" who made the first move towards segregation. I'm quite sure it was instinctive and sheep-like on all sides. It would have been comical if it had not been so miserably stupid. Fortunately, with the issue of uniforms and the disappearance of most of the class and income labels that we display in civilian life, we all became the best of friends, helping each other into the unfamiliar and complicated naval rig and strutting up and down like a covey of mannequins. Kitting-up and some square-bashing knocked us into a common pattern, and it was not until a fortnight later, when we moved on to the seamanship course on *H.M.S. Ganges*, at Shotley Barracks, Ipswich, that individual identities began to emerge again. Then the sheep were separated from the goats, the men from the boys, the sailors from the lubbers.

Like many other people, I have never managed to learn how to learn. Sitting at a desk and trying to soak up knowledge is a pursuit that I find as difficult as it is unrewarding. I cannot convince myself that it is really doing anything. Consequently, ninety per cent of the seamanship course floated straight over my head – helped by the fact that I had found something much more interesting to think about.

Towards the end of the second week at *H.M.S. Royal Arthur*, we had been told that it was usual for each course to put on a ship's concert. Fortified by my considerable experience in the entertainment world (variety at Haslemere, drama at Brixton – to say nothing of intimate cabaret in Aunt Belle's sitting-room) I volunteered to organise it. I also contributed my impersonations and found that they went down as well as they had done at Haslemere. I was still far from considering ever doing this sort of thing professionally, but I enjoyed the applause and was eager for any opportunity to get more practice.

So when I arrived at *H.M.S Ganges* I leaped at an invitation to do a turn in the petty officers' mess. In fact, I did one nearly every week. They very politely kept asking me, and I very gratefully kept going back. The result of all this extra-curricular activity was that in the intervals between dreaming about beautiful Wrens, I was usually either thinking up new impersonations or snatching a quiet and recuperative forty winks.

Out of a sense of duty, or just to raise a laugh, an instructor would occasionally say "Jacobs is the only man present who could answer that one," and rouse me with a well-aimed box of matches or a piece of chalk. My startled look at being jerked back to consciousness – followed by one of sheer stupefaction when the question was repeated – was always greeted with applause. I was possibly the most widely and warmly appreciated dunce ever to pass through *H.M.S Ganges*. But I still had to face the seamanship examination at the end of the course, and as it grew nearer my face grew glummer. It is one thing to win friends and entertain people by being stupid in the comparative privacy of a classroom, but quite another thing to have a list stuck up on a very public notice board ending: "Jacobs D. – 0". It is the sort of thing that gets put into an official return and forwarded to the Admiralty; the sort of thing that historians ferret out after a couple of centuries and have a lot of ponderous fun with. I didn't want to appear in the Historical Quarterly for September 2144, festooned with footnotes and headed "Jacobs, D., the Idiot Ordinary Seaman; fresh light on the only recruit to score 0 out of 600 in a mid-twentieth century seamanship course." And there were even a few contemporaries, Wrens included, who might get a nasty giggle out of it.

I was feeling very pessimistic when I presented myself to the first petty-officer examiner. He picked up a piece of rope and said, "Jacobs, will you please show me how to tie a granny knot?" I could scarcely believe my ears. It was well-known locally that the Granny Knot was shortly to be renamed the Jacobs Knot: no matter what knot, bend, hitch or nautical ligature I was called upon to demonstrate, I would infallibly come up with a granny.

I did as I had been asked, and the petty-officer said, "Fine. Absolutely first class." I was then ushered along to the next examiner, who was to probe my knowledge of the parts of a ship. He laid the tip of his finger on the pointed end of the model in front of him and said, "Tell me, Jacobs, what do you call this in the Navy?"

There was evidently a catch in it, but I could think of no other reply, so I said, with a hesitant lift to my voice: "Bows?"

"Yes," said the examiner. "The bows. very Good indeed. Now just one more question: have you any idea what we call this?" He slid his finger along to the other end of the ship.

"The stern, sir," I said very firmly.

"Excellent," said the examiner.

And so it went on as I passed from one satisfied examiner to the next, and it gradually dawned on me that the petty-officers were having a little fun and perhaps repaying me for the evenings I had spent trying to entertain them in their mess. Each of them carried the joke through with gusto and without much reference to his colleagues, so that, when the results were published there was Jacobs, D. at the top of the list with 600 out of 600. I was even presented with a bosun's whistle.

The ten recruits who passed out at the head of the course were automatically considered for training for a commission. I stopped thinking up new impersonations for the petty-officers' mess and began to contemplate my imminent elevation to the upper deck. My dreams went widescreen and technicoloured: Midshipman Jacobs, all gold lace (or was it only gold buttons to start with?), peaked cap, ceremonial dirk, starched white cuffs –

and rows of enamoured Wrens swooning into the distance. It was not until I went for my interview with the commanding officers that I realised that the Navy had not really gone out of its great big nautical mind.

"Jacobs," he said. "Your examination results were remarkable. I cannot recall any man ever getting 600 out of 600 on this course before. Absolutely first class."

I said "Thank you, sir," and tried not to look to conceited. I was by this time prepared to be convinced that I had really earned my 600 marks. After all, I had answered all the questions they had asked me.

"You have excelled in your seamanship course," the commanding officer continued, "and I do not need to tell you that what the Navy needs above all else is good seamen." He paused. "I have therefore decided that you shall remain a good seaman."

SIR YEHUDI MENUHIN

The Parcel

I have repeatedly been asked to talk about memories I have of my experiences during the war when I performed in various parts of the world in the hope to give comfort to those listening. Out of a myriad of impressions, two stand out – two of a very different kind.

When I played with Benjamin Britten, who was able to express some of his recollections in his War Requiem, at Bergen-Belsen, my main aim was to rekindle hope in those human beings who had been spared a most terrible death and who had a new life ahead of them.

At another time, I played for American soldiers in Hawaii who were to be flown to the Pacific frontline the following day to fight against the Japanese. They, contrary to the people at Belsen, had death right in front of their eyes. There was no thought of heroism, no comfort in the belief to be safe in God's hands, as apparently the children of Iran can experience before going to fight. My heart was very heavy at that time.

A few years ago a parcel was left for me at the stage door of a concert hall. No sender was given. On opening it I found an old album, containing shellac recordings of my Bach Sonatas

140

recording for unaccompanied violin. The man who gave this present to me had written inside the tattered cover simply this "Your recordings accompanied me everywhere during the war years travelling in my pack. Wherever I managed to locate a gramophone, I would play them. They kept me safe and sane. Now I feel I should return them to their rightful owner."

I am forever sad not to be able to thank this man; he could not have given me a greater gift.

HOW YOU AND 'THE STARS' ARE CONTRIBUTING TO SERVICES FOR PEOPLE WITH AUTISM.

Do you remember the Oscar winning film *Rain Man* in which Dustin Hoffman and Tom Cruise starred? If so, you will recall Hoffman's superb portrayal of the main character in the film, an autistic man called Raymond.

Raymond is diagnosed by the medical profession as being an "Autistic Savant". He suffers from an inability to communicate meaningfully, to understand human relationships and general concepts such as money and, as a result, is unable to live happily outside a mental institution. You will recall also from the film that Raymond has an exceptional mental dexterity for number work which leads to his brother making a considerable amount of money from card games in Las Vegas.

Whilst it is true that some autisic people, like Raymond, do have very special talents in specific areas, it is equally true to say that the majority of people with autism have very severe learning disabilities and have very poorly developed self-help and social skills. What charcterises all autistic people is an overwhelming anxiety when confronted with situations that they cannot understand. Under such circumstances autistic people require understanding and considerable reassurance.

"Autism Europe" has predicted that there are 80,000 children and adults living in England and Wales who are autistic or have autistic features, yet for adults there are currently less than 500 available places within specialist autistic communities.

The West Midland Autistic Society Ltd, which is affiliated to the National Autistic Society, was formed by parents with autistic children some years ago and now provides advice and support for parents in a similar position. The Society constantly strives to develop the support they can give to families, and their mission has been exemplified by the establishment, in 1989, of the Oakfield House Autistic Community, the first specialist community for adults with autism in the West Midlands region. The facilities provided by Oakfield House are widely recognised as being of enormous value and quality, yet this provision is just a drop in the ocean, so far as autistic poeple and their families in the West Midlands are concerned.

By buying this book you have helped to provide badly-needed services for children and adults with autism, as well as having a darned good read.

Hugh Morgan.